About the Author

Nell Carpenter is an adoptive parent of two sisters, Rosie and Annie. Nell firmly believes nurturing parenting practices, along with firm boundaries and a great deal of self-reflection and ability to adapt can lead to happy, contented children. Nell's early career working as a family therapist in Multi Systemic Therapy ultimately led her to adopting her own children eight years later.

Someday This Could be Ordinary…
Our Adoption Journey

Learning, Loss, Love & Laughs

Nell Carpenter

_____

–

Someday This Could be Ordinary…
Our Adoption Journey

Learning, Loss, Love & Laughs

Vanguard Press

VANGUARD PAPERBACK

© Copyright 2024
Nell Carpenter

The right of Nell Carpenter to be identified as author of
this work has been asserted by her in accordance with the
Copyright, Designs and Patents Act 1988.

All Rights Reserved

No reproduction, copy or transmission of this publication
may be made without written permission.
No paragraph of this publication may be reproduced,
copied or transmitted save with the written permission of the
publisher, or in accordance with the provisions
of the Copyright Act 1956 (as amended).

Any person who commits any unauthorised act in relation to
this publication may be liable to criminal
prosecution and civil claims for damages.

A CIP catalogue record for this title is
available from the British Library.

ISBN 978 1 83794 099 8

Vanguard Press is an imprint of
Pegasus Elliot Mackenzie Publishers Ltd.
www.pegasuspublishers.com

First Published in 2024

Vanguard Press
Sheraton House Castle Park
Cambridge England

Printed & Bound in Great Britain

To every parent who has ever experienced that 'Mum guilt'. You are not alone. You are doing great.

I would like to thank, from the bottom of my heart, every family member and friend who has offered kind words of wisdom, encouragement and no judgement throughout this journey, right from the moment we decided to adopt and up to this point. I would also like to thank the social workers of Barnardo's Scotland who supported us throughout the process and were passionate about providing us with effective support and ensuring we got the best match possible. Most of all, I would like to thank my children, who are the apple of my eye, my vital teachers who have taught me more about resilience, perseverance and determination than any expert ever could.

Introduction

It's been seven weeks since we brought the girls home for the first time. Some days it feels like two weeks and some days it feels like two years. So many people warned me how tiring it would be and how exhausted I would feel. I naively thought I have been exhausted before; I will be fine. Boy was I wrong. I honestly look like death wrapped up. The mental, emotional and physical exhaustion I experienced particularly in the first month of the girls moving in with us is like *nothing* I have ever experienced. It was just constant. I thought getting our little cockapoo Angus as an eight-week-old puppy was tiring but comparing that to bringing home an eight-year-old and a three-year-old with their own little personalities having come from a lifetime of trauma, chaos and disruption and trying to merge as a brand-new family, well it's no comparison really. Nothing prepared me for how I would feel. No matter how many times a social worker spoke about it or how often I read it in books or listened to podcasts; until you live it, you can't comprehend it. Today I decided I wanted to write down my experience of our adoption journey and share the highs and the lows, the ugly and the beautiful, the grim and extraordinary.

I have this app on my phone where positive and motivational quotes are sent to me a few times a day. Yesterday's quote was, *One day you will tell your story of how you overcame what you went through and it will be someone else's survival guide.*" Let's hope what I have written might be useful to other adopters, extended family members of adopters, professionals involved in adoption and of course anyone who is interested in the crazy journey we have embarked on. I have written with complete honesty and openness. I don't want to glamourise our experience. It has been really tough; it has changed me as a person. But they do say smooth seas do not make skilful sailors…

Chapter 1

Why Adoption?

It's 2015…

I have always known I wanted a family. Kit and I have only been dating a few months and I broach the 'do you want kids?' sooner than most people probably would in their dating journey. There are twelve years between Kit and I and I am a little bit worried that I will fall head over heels and then find out we don't have the same hopes and dreams for the future. I am nervous throwing the question out there, but I can't help myself, this is an important one for me. I really have no idea what she will say. She has lived a very independent, commitment-free lifestyle for so long that I'm just not sure what her vision for the future looks like.

"Do you see yourself having kids and a family?" I say as we were sat drinking a cup of tea on a sunny Saturday morning in my flat on Leith Walk.

She replies, "To be honest I had never really thought about it and never really thought it would happen but I would love to have kids if there was the opportunity to." Her face lights up. I am surprised and happy with her response. I have always seen myself with kids and being married and I'm beyond delighted to find out that she wants the same things.

I am working as a Multi Systemic Therapist (MST), started the job back in 2013 and it is just the best job I have ever had. I remember going for the interview and thinking I would never get the job. I loved the sound of it but I wasn't convinced they would see me as qualified enough. To be honest, I wasn't exactly qualified for it, but I was young, super keen, focused and wanting to make a difference. I think they took a lucky swing with hiring me, and thankfully, it worked out. One of the supervisors, Beth, is like the MST Queen. She is only thirty but her knowledge of MST and behaviour therapy and parenting practices and her approach to the job is second to none. I am learning so much from her and she makes me want to be the best and do the best. Working as an MST therapist is one of the most challenging yet rewarding jobs I've ever done. I have the opportunity to work with families to support parents with behaviour management and support young people to stop engaging in high-risk behaviours and essentially bring the family members together to create a positive, nurturing and safe environment. I meet so many parents at the end of their tether, feeling hopeless and powerless in the situation they find themselves in with their child's behaviour out of their control. What a high I get when I am able to embed myself into the family unit and help parents regain control, instil nurturing parenting practices and bring families back together again. I just love seeing parents' confidence growing in their abilities to set boundaries and follow through and then the knock-on effect of the child's behaviour improving and parents wanting to reward their children and spend time with them. It is just a magical process to watch. Right before my eyes I get to watch love blossom again. It isn't always a happy ending of course. There are some parents that aren't able to, for lots of different reasons, develop more nurturing parenting practices and keep their children safe. These are the cases that really tug at my heart strings. There's one boy Sam who I am working with. He is fourteen, coming up for fifteen and lives at home with his mum and his mum's boyfriend. He has three younger sisters and an older sister. The three younger sisters (all under four) were removed from the care of Mum and were adopted by other families. The older sister moved out when she was sixteen. It is only Sam left at home. He was referred to MST because there had been several police reports about behaviour in the community and non-school attendance. I am expecting to meet a boy that will have a serious attitude problem and hate the idea of MST getting involved in his life. What I find is the polar opposite. His relationship with his mum is so strained and non-existent. In the house, no one speaks to him unless they need him to do something like go to the shop for cigarettes, take the bin out or make a cup of tea. Sam is a little boy who is feeling alone and desperate for his mum to bother about him. The good thing about this case is Mum actually allows me in to visit. She has a long history of non-engagement with services. I am like a dog with a bone trying to make sure I manage to keep getting through the door. I learn a great deal about Sam's mum. She has experienced so much trauma in her own childhood, it has really impacted her own abilities to parent or even develop into a healthy functioning adult. She very much functions like a teenager and is stuck in survival mode. I try everything in my power to support her; be more involved, more nurturing, more present, but she just isn't able to sustain the changes. I realise I am failing in this case as Sam starts to rely on me more and more. He calls me on my mobile and tells me he missed the bus because Mum hasn't woke him up and asks me to give him a lift. I go and pick him up and go into the house. I find Mum comatose on the couch. He tells me that he is starving because Mum has put all the food in the locked fridge that's in her own bedroom. It just isn't okay for Sam to be living like this. I am a great MST therapist but I'm not a miracle maker. I know it's now was time to call it quits, it is time to help the social worker gather information for the children's hearing panel for Sam to live somewhere where his needs can be met. Despite the strained relationship and the passive role his mum plays, Sam is fiercely loyal to his mum. When out of the earshot of his mum, Sam is excited at the idea of going to live in a children's home but Sam doesn't dare speak out of turn in front of his mum. We go to visit the children's home, he is bought a new pair of white Nike trainers by his key worker and I've never seen a kid so thrilled about a pair of shoes. They become his prized possession.

The children's panel is hard. Mum and her boyfriend are over an hour late and are then invited in. One of the panel members asks Sam where he wants to live. The feeling of anxiety in my stomach as I watch how torn Sam is. *Why are they putting the pressure on Sam to answer? Surely the Social Work Recommendations are enough. Putting him on the spot like this feels so unfair.* He doesn't want to hurt his mum; his whole life he has tried to protect her. I can see how hard it is for him. He looks over at me, he doesn't say a word but I feel he is asking, 'what should I say'.

I give him a reassuring nod and a smile and then he says quickly in an aggressive tone, "The home." Mum starts shouting and swearing at the professionals and gets up and leaves the room. It is the only way Mum knows how to navigate through this, she has to blame someone. Sam looks scared. His world as he knows it has just shattered into a million pieces. He's probably never felt more alone than he does in this room at this point. The Children's Panel made the right decision. No one ever wants to remove children from the care of their birth parents but ultimately Sam's safety and well-being had to be the priority. The panel members wish him well and he gets up to head straight to the home with the social worker. I walk him to the car with the social worker. My involvement stops here. My heart feels heavy. I make a joke about keeping his white trainers clean and setting his alarm clock for school and wave goodbye as they drive off. I don't feel good about this case. I feel like Sam has been let down by the system. I have so many unanswered questions. Why was he not removed when his little sisters were? Why was he not given the option of being adopted to a loving family? Why do foster carers not take him? Why was he left in this life? Sam's case has never left me and ultimately his story would change the direction of my life forever.

Chapter 2

The Intrauterine Insemination Part

It's 2017. Kit and I get engaged and the wedding is booked for July 2018. We speak about expanding and having kids and decide to go private and get fertility tests done. Kit is forty-two and is already thinking herself she is passed the point of being able to get pregnant, I am only twenty-nine so I'm feeling quite hopeful. I am fit and healthy. I'm feeling so excited about going for the fertility tests. I think to myself *How lucky are we. We will likely get pregnant really quickly and we are both female so surely one of us will be really fertile.* We go to the clinic and get the blood tests and are asked to come back for a meeting with the doctor the following week to discuss the results.

I say to Kit, "I think we are really lucky; we will get pregnant really quickly." We are both naturally positive and optimistic people so haven't really thought about it not being easy. A week passes and we are back at the clinic and feeling really quite nervous. It all feels very clinical and really impersonal. I really didn't like it. I can't even tell you what the consultant looks like. He doesn't have great eye contact and keeps his eyes on the written report in front of him for the majority of our meeting.

"For your age, you are very low on the fertility scale Nell. A healthy range is between fifteen to thirty and you are 11.5. Kit you are 0.5 so wouldn't be viable for IVF." He was so very matter-of-fact about the whole thing. He goes on to say, "I wouldn't be recommending IUI for you Nell and feel IVF is the option you need in order to give you a chance to conceive successfully."

I stop listening to him after that. He says a great deal more and uses a lot of big fancy words that I probably can't even spell. All I can think is, *I don't know if I want to put myself through this.* We thank the doctor and leave the building. We are both so silent on the outside but no doubt Kit's mind is racing just as much as mine. We get into the car and then the tears come. Kit is still trying to be so upbeat. She is still being really positive and optimistic.

"People get pregnant all the time and don't know if they are fertile. Let's still try the IUI. You just never know. It could be that 1% chance that we conceive." Her words definitely make me feel better but there is a big part of me that isn't feeling quite as optimistic about the whole thing as she is. I never want to let her down or be a Debbie Downer though so I jump on the 'let's do this train' to see where we will get to.

We decide to pay the extra for the European sperm donor bank as there are a lot more choice. It feels odd going through profiles to pick sperm to make a child with a complete stranger and the fact that we were doing it sitting on the couch eating popcorn makes it ever more surreal. Both of us struggle with this concept but us being us fully emersed ourselves into the process. We pick a doner and fill out all the forms and before we know it, we are booked in for the insemination.

The ten-day waiting period is a killer. You convince yourself you are pregnant, only to experience the disappointment when they call to say it hasn't worked. After the two 'not this time' phone calls I think I can't do this. I am also going through a rough time at work with a new manager and I am starting to question whether I am trying to get pregnant because I really think the time is right or if it is to get away from her and I really don't want to be a person that has a baby for the wrong reasons. So, we have a break for a year or so. We buy a house, get our puppy, Angus, get married, the first house is old and freezing so we buy a new house, a lovely new-build that is warm, I get a new job, we go on a big adventure for our honeymoon—New Zealand, Australia, Bali – all the usual milestones. Throughout this time thinking about kids never leaves me but the more I think about it, the more the idea of adoption keeps creeping into my thoughts. Sam's story is always at the back of my mind. I wonder how many Sam's are out there that need a loving family?

After life comes to a natural pause, Kit and I chat about how we will get to the next stage and what would be the best path for us. We are driving in the car going to IKEA, it's Saturday afternoon so traffic is quite busy. This is the moment I drop the bomb of wanting to adopt. Kit's face is a picture. After I try my hardest to explain my reasons and my thoughts around it, I can see she is more open to the idea, but being a business woman with no real knowledge or experience in this field I know it is a stretch for her. It is after this first conversation that adoption starts to feel like our first option over anything else. For us, we want an end result, we want to be parents. When we explore the concept further, Kit says she would feel more 'part of it' if we adopt because then neither of us would be biologically related and we would have a story to tell our adopted children about their background. It is kind of a like 'the penny dropped' moment and it feels so right that adoption would be the best option for us.

Chapter 3

The Long Drawn-out Adoption Process

2019.
I make the first phone call to Barnardo's and they arrange for the first social worker to come do our first assessment. Her name is Lesley, she is really nice and puts us at ease. It feels so funny to be on the other side. I'm normally the professional going into people's home. It makes me realise how intrusive it can feel for people. We have cleaned the house from top to bottom, we paid the dog walker to take Angus out for double the time so he wouldn't have one of his crazy moments when the social worker is here. Yet despite the extra walk, Angus still decides to have a crazy turn and starts trying to play fight with Kit on the couch in the middle of our discussions with Lesley. To people who aren't used to dogs it can look quite aggressive. I get up and take Angus

and put him in his bed and tell him to stay (trying to show that I have some sort of authority). As I sit back on the couch, Angus comes bounding back to the couch to start play fighting again. My plan to look like I'm in control of my own dog has not worked. I decide to make a joke about Angus showing us up in front of Lesley and thankfully she laughs with us. It puts us at ease again. To be fair to Angus she has been sitting asking us questions for over two and a half hours by this point. After she gathered every bit of information about our upbringing, our jobs, our past experiences and our finances it was a wrap. We are now scheduled to take part in the adoption prep group that is taking place in Jan 2020.

Prep group is the best part of the process for us. Getting to meet other people who are adopting and getting to listen to other people who have adopted is super helpful. There are two mums who come to do a talk on their experience. One mum has adopted three kids who are all teenagers now and one mum has recently in the last year adopted a little boy and has a biological son too. Hearing the reality of what life is like is great. They are both super honest but I can also tell how much they love their kids and wouldn't change it for the world. This fills us with hope for our own match. The prep group is run over three days. We get into a WhatsApp group with the other adopters for a peer support network so we can keep each other updated on our matches.

It's now March 2020, I haven't heard anything from social work but I'm assured the process just takes time. I am not a woman who handles things in a slow fashion. Once I've made my mind up on something then I like to take action to make it happen immediately. This process is going to be testing for me. My mobile rings when I'm at work, private number so I answer straight away. It's a social worker called Ali. She sounds lovely. She tells me she has been allocated to us and will be doing our home stay study which will last over twenty weeks. *I think to myself twenty weeks, is she kiddin?* She goes on to say, at the end of the assessment, she writes a big report about us and that's then sent to the social workers of children that are on the adoption register and they use that information to determine if we will be a good match. Unfortunately for us the week we are scheduled to have our first visit from Ali, the world goes into a national lockdown due to Covid-19. Ali calls me back and luckily we are still going ahead with our assessment but will start off via Skype. For the next twenty weeks we meet with Ali virtually every Friday from four p.m. to six p.m. A lot of the things we talk about are things we have already went through with Lesley, the very first social worker that came to do the first visit, but we just go into a lot more detail. I actually really enjoy our meetings with Ali. I think it helps that we can't make any plans like we normally would because we are in lockdown so it is something to look forward to. Ali has a warm and friendly manner and we both really click with her. I think it would feel very different if we hadn't clicked with her and then had to talk about every aspect of ourselves with someone we don't like. Having the rapport with Ali is really important for me. Don't get me wrong, she leaves no table unturned. She even contacts our exes for a reference. I don't have many exes but I could have kicked myself that the latest ex was the one that I didn't talk to. Fortunately, all is fine and the reference was done, but I'm so sure Helz or Jenny would have made me sound so much better.

The whole process makes me overanalyse and worry about every little thing. I don't have a relationship with my own birth dad. My mum split from him before I was even two years old and I could count on one hand how many times I've seen him in my childhood but the irrational worry that goes through my head about him is ridiculous. When I was a teenager, he spent time in prison and I manage to convince myself one night when I can't sleep that Ali will find this out and decide we won't be suitable to adopt because I'm the daughter of a criminal drug dealer. It's incredible what my mind can jump to when I can't sleep. On another night, after speaking about the time I went to counselling after my nana died because I had struggled because I had been the one to find her on Christmas Day, I convinced myself they would think I wasn't mentally tough or stable enough to cope so wouldn't let us adopt. Turns out, all these personal experiences I had to share are written in our report as positives. Ali put a positive spin on all of it. She wrote how I reached out for support after my nana died and used my support network and how that quality would be transferable to parenting, and reaching out for support if things were tough is an important thing to do. She highlighted my attachments to my mum and my nana and how I had trusting secure relationships and I knew the difference between good parenting and absent parenting. I am amazed to see that actually it didn't matter what had happened in my life but it was how I responded to it and how I processed it that mattered. That's what makes me who I am. That's what makes me an approved adopter.

It's now May and we are going to the approval panel. It is virtual because of Covid, so we get to sit in the comfort of our own house at our kitchen table. It is a weird experience with social workers in little boxes on the laptop screen asking us questions about our report. It feels like a tick-box exercise and we would have had to have said something really out there for them not to approve us, but you still can't help feeling apprehensive, just in case. Thankfully ten minutes after the virtual meeting ended Ali calls us to confirm we have officially been approved. We decide to go to the local café down at the beach and get a massive ice cream sundae to celebrate. I can't help but wonder just how long it will then take us to find out who our child will be.

The following day I get access to the adoption register UK. I literally zoom home from work on my bike to get in and get on. I have technically difficulties but luckily one of the workers at Barnardos is able to talk me through how to log on before she finishes for the day. There are over 600 children on the register. I am astounded by the amount of sibling groups. Something that really stuck with me from the prep group was hearing the social worker say children over the age of four are often classed as 'unadoptable' because they are seen as too old. The number of kids on the register over four years old is way more than half the kids. Seeing this makes me want to adopt a sibling group. We naively had this vision that we would adopt one and then a year or two later adopt another, but we quickly realise that adoption doesn't quite work like that. If you want more than one then you need to take the siblings together at the same time. Unfortunately, Ali had left to another job so we have a new social worker. Her name is Ange. She is retired but has come back to help out. I am apprehensive, we had got on so well with Ali, it was hard to imagine going through the process with someone else, but I really like Ange. She is quirky and she really knows her stuff. She does sessions with us about siblings. She is good at challenging our thinking and shifting our naivety. We get a slot to go back to the approval panel in August to be approved from adopting not just one child, but two.

I go through so many children's profiles sometimes over and over again. There is one sibling group, two girls, a five-year-old and a two-year-old. We go to a meeting with the social worker and the foster carers. I can't explain it but it just doesn't feel like the right match. Some of the information we are asking for we are getting really vague answers and it felt like they are trying to hide how hard it is to manage their behaviours. I don't sleep a wink and I go to work and can't stop thinking about it. I thought if I feel like they are keeping things from us already then it doesn't bode well for moving forward and all working really closely with each other. These kids also live only fourteen miles away from us, as does birth mum. It just doesn't feel right. I dread having to explain to Kit. I get home and feel awful but have to say to Kit that it just doesn't feel like it is the right match for us. I can't put it into words but it is just a gut feeling that it isn't right. For a few weeks I feel a bit deflated. It's a few days before Christmas, I go back onto link maker and I find a new profile. The profile has videos and photos. I watch and rewatch the videos over and over. I am so taken by the older child, she is seven. She has beautiful, long, dark hair. There is a video of her playing a tune on the piano and then of her colouring in a love heart and giving it to the foster carer and she says, "That's for your family," as she looks up and smiles.

The younger girl is three years old and there is a video of her playing with playdough. She is so cute and cheeky looking. I am instantly drawn to them. I show Kit the videos and I can tell she is instantly taken too. I send an email 'noting interest'. That expression doesn't sit well with me but that's what it's called. On Christmas Eve I get an email back from the social work manager to tell me the allocated social worker is off on leave but she would send over the girls' reports for us to read through and the social worker would be back in touch after the holiday period. The report is forty-five pages long. It is not for easy reading. These little humans have not had an easy start in life and have been through so much already. I just know then that these little beauties are meant to be with us. It is a weird, quiet Christmas and New Year. I'm not a very patient person and navigating through such a slow process has pained me. I just try to keep myself busy. People keep telling me to enjoy the quiet time cause once there are kids there isn't any quiet time.

I keep saying, "I'm ready to fill that quiet time with noise." I will probably look back and laugh at myself for not enjoying the quiet when the kids do come along and wish that I had treasured the quiet time but as my mum says, "There's nae tellin ye," and she's right, I am not listening to anyone. I just have one focus, one desire and that is to adopt these two tiny little humans.

2020 comes to an end and 2021 is when it all starts to move (although still not at the speed I would have liked). There are several teams' meetings with social workers discussing the potential match and then they have to come and visit the house to assess us in person and inspect the home. The girls' social worker is called Ruth. We really like her. She is really invested in the girls and I can tell she is really fond of them and wants what is best for them. We have to go back to a third approval panel because we are only approved for children under the age of seven and Rosie turned eight in January, so that's added yet another unnecessary delay. One important thing for me is that I want to meet the girls' birth mum. I had always said right from the beginning that we needed to do this as it would be important for us and important for the girls to know too. Fortunately the girls birth Mum was willing to meet with us. It has to be done over teams because of Covid rules. It is really nerve-wracking. She is with Ruth, the social worker in the social work office and we are in our kitchen at home. Our third social worker who is now supporting us, Alice, is also present and she has logged on from her home too. I notice straight away that Michelle, the girls birth mum has beautiful dark hair and a bubbly warm personality. I instantly warm to her. She asks us a list of questions about ourselves. It kind of feels like we are being interviewed at first, but I can imagine she probably feels just as nervous as us. I tell her a bit about my job and work I've done with young people and tell her about my beloved camper van, Betsy which she thinks is funny.

She turns to Ruth and says, "They two are funny." I ask her what her hopes for the girls are which then leads the meeting to the more emotional point. She says she wants them to be safe and have a happy childhood. She is so honest and really owns her mistakes which makes me really respect her.

She says, "I know I've made a lot of mistakes but I love my babies and I just want them to be happy and safe."

I start to tear up at this point and I say, "We don't ever want to try and replace you, Michelle. You will always be their birth mum and we will keep you alive in their stories. I promise you we will give them so much love and protect and take care of them."

She then says, "I'm just so happy it's you two. I've not been treated well by men my whole life and I feel good that they will have two women taking care of them." The meeting lasts a good hour and a half. It is the most powerful emotional meeting I think I've ever been part of. Anyone who goes through the process, I would always recommend meeting birth parents. You can get trapped in the forty-five-page report that has all the hard, bad stuff that happened that you don't get to hear what some of the positive parts of their life were. We found out that Michelle had taken them on holiday, we found out how she picked their names and we saw first-hand that there was without a doubt love for her children underneath all the mistakes. This meeting will be crucial in conversations with Rosie and Annie further down the line.

We eventually go to matching panel in May 2021 and are delighted to be matched with the girls. The complexities with the adoption order legal process is mind-blowing. Nothing is simple or indeed the way it had originally been described. We are told if we don't do a direct petition route for adoption through court system, then the girls will need to stay in foster care until that happens which could be another year to eighteen months. So of course, by this point, we don't want any delays, Rosie has already turned eight. We are reassured the process will be smooth as birth mum has agreed to the adoption route and it will be plain sailing. We also don't want to do a direct petition because we never wanted it to be or feel like it was us fighting against birth mum to get the care of her children. We met Michelle and are happy with how it went, we don't want the legal process to jeopardise that.

We eventually get to meet the girls in person on the first weekend of July 2021. We have to drive up north to meet them at their foster carers house and spend a few hours with them on the Saturday and the Sunday. The whole thing feels surreal. I feel like I am watching from the outside and someone else is in control of my body. As soon as we park up in the driveway, Rosie comes running out to hug us and Annie comes running out copying her. They are very over-familiar but I don't worry about it too much as it makes the first meeting so much easier. They both have little summer dresses on and Annie has her hair in breads and Rosie has her long hair up in a half-pony. We play with them the whole day. We were so worried that it would be awkward and strained but it isn't. The social worker wasn't lying when she had told us that Rosie was so excited to have a family, I can really see it now. We go back up the following weekend and spend time with them again with respite foster carers and then we have a break the following weekend as I am bridesmaid for my best friend, Davina's wedding then we go up for a full week and stay in an apartment beside the foster carers house whilst spending every day with them and then they officially move in with us on the 26th of July 2021. The transition week is exhausting, being in someone else's house trying to parent two children you don't know is awkward to say the least, plus the behaviours are all so new to us. It is easy talking about how we intended to deal with things but now the reality of it all was kicking in.

Chapter 4

The Strangest Week of my Life

The week spent in Freda; the foster carers house is honestly the hardest week of my life. Everything is so strange. The whole set-up feels odd. In what other situation would you be going into someone else's house that you don't know and taking over their role? I find it entirely uncomfortable. It was described to us as if it would be an empowering process and it would be our chance to watch and then gradually copy and take over from the foster carer in their daily routines. In reality we watch one night of bedtime routine and then are thrown in at the deep end for the rest of the week. I'm not sure if this is the intention or if this is unique to our experience. The first night of us doing the bedtime routine is what I can only describe as a disaster. I put Annie to bed and Kit put Rosie to bed while Freda sits at her dining table on her laptop quietly listening to the chaos unfold. Annie has an absolute meltdown, wrecks the room completely. What should have taken thirty minutes takes me four hours. Rosie isn't as challenging as Annie but she tests the water in a different way in what she is saying to Kit. One of the days we took them to a trampoline park and Annie had another meltdown because she demanded a slushie and I said no. Next day we take them to the park and Annie demands a second ice cream and I say no which creates an almighty meltdown. We are noticing a bit of a theme. Annie's meltdowns are like nothing I have ever dealt with. Kit and I spend a lot of time biting our tongue as we watch different situations unfold and seeing the way Freda responds, particularly with Annie. I understand that it is sometimes easier to say yes but I could also see that it was creating a monster. Her behaviour appeared to be very functional to me, i.e., if I kick off big time they will give in and I will get what I want. Freda is a very nurturing, loving lady and the kids adore her, it is very obvious they have an attachment to her which is positive to see. Even though I have never parented before, I just knew I was going to be completely different and will be different in my approach to situations compared to Freda. This makes me worry about what the future will look like. I feel like Annie gets to dictate what is going on a lot of the time and it looks like she has not really experienced the word no. I knew I didn't want to live my life feeling on edge or being scared to say no to her just in case she has a meltdown. Kit and I talk and agree we will be adopting our own style. We need to be true to ourselves. I know my personality and approach to life is the polar opposite to Freda. I am really glad to get to the end of the week and to be heading to my own home to start life the way I want. I can't wait to just get on with it in my own way. I feel grateful to Freda. It couldn't have been easy for her to have two strangers in her house taking over her role of taking care of the kids she has loved and taken care of for eighteen months. I will always be thankful that Freda took care of them so well and showed them so much warmth and love. But it is now my turn.

Chapter 5

The Loneliness You Don't Expect

Before we got the kids, I remember thinking how will I feel lonely when we have a busy house full of chaos, noise, chatter and busyness? How can I possibly feel lonely? I just didn't get it when other parents or social workers spoke about it. The answer I now know is that 'you absolutely can and will feel the loneliest you have felt for such a long time'. Starting from the transition up to Freda's to bringing them home and it just being the four of us has been so tough. You have a vision in your head and in actual fact the reality is very different. The first few months we are told to just spend time, the four of us, embedding as a family and then gradually introduce extended family members. Not seeing my mum or my friends for the first weeks has been so much tougher than I imagined. Kit's dad is also terminally ill so Kit has been away a lot helping her mum with her dad. Despite the advice from social work we take the kids to meet Kit's Dad. We know the kids will probably be over stimulated but we feel it's the right thing to do. We know he doesn't have long and time is not on our side. We get there and Annie climbs up onto his knee straight away and he is very taken by her, she's very curious about his plasters and asks him if she can have one. She cuddles into him, almost like she knows she has to be gentle with him. I'm so glad he is getting to see Kit being a mum. James passed away a few weeks later. It's a real emotional and tough time. I can't imagine how Kit feels having to deal with the grief of losing a parent right at the time she is establishing her role as becoming a parent herself. Kit is a very deep person and doesn't say much but I can see it in her. Naturally she retreats and goes into herself as she deals with the loss of her dad. Being on my own with the girls when Kit is away helping her Mum is probably my darkest times. I am so exhausted, don't really have a clue what I am doing and their behaviours are still really unsettled and challenging. I have the up most respect for single adopters who take two children. My mum comes to visit and get to know the kids. She stays for a few days. I have a mixed bag of emotions with her visiting. I just felt so relieved she is coming but also so nervous and anxious due to the unsettled behaviours of the girls. We go for a walk with the dogs, the kids run on to the play park. I just burst into tears, I am exhausted, mentally, emotionally and physically and just feel like I am doing a shit job and wondering if it will ever feel better.

My mum puts her arms round me and I will never forget what she says next, "Nell, this is really hard. This whole transition has been awful for you both, but it's also completely normal to feel like this. A lot of new mums bring their babies home from the hospital and just can't cope . It will get better. You are doing such an amazing job. You don't have to pretend it's easy or it isn't a struggle. People will be expecting you to say that it has been really hard. You have brought home two little personalities into your family and you need to get to know them plus all the complexities of the social work stuff with birth family and James dying and Kit grieving. I love you and I'm so proud of you." Just letting my tears out and being held by my Mum is such a release. I have been trying so hard to keep it together and be the strong one when Kit is dealing with her dad's illness and then him passing away, but I realise having a cry and being honest and still getting up every day and trying to make the next day better and learn from mistakes is still being strong, it just didn't feel like it at the time. I am desperate to get to the point where I can use my family and friends for more support. It is just so lonely building the bonds of attachment without them fully being part of the process. I know it difficult for them too. I didn't really think about how hard it would be when we talked about it with the social worker. The reality of it all kicked in pretty much the first day of the transition. I didn't think about how I would feel being around social workers and the foster carer in the first hard moments. All my other hard moments in life I have relied heavily on my close friends and family.

Chapter 6

The Start of School and Nursery

Rosie is beyond excited to start school. There were lots of debates about whether she should wait and start school later as she had only been with us for four weeks before the school term started, but she was so desperate to start and make new friends. She was so desperate to be normal and the idea of having her first day of P4 with everyone else being in the same boat on their first day was important to her. She really wanted to fit in. So, we listened to her and decided it was best to let her start sooner rather than later. Plus, she had this desperate need to know about everything in her new life. I take her round to see the school building a few days before she is due to start. The school is only a few minutes' walk from our house. The gates are open so I take her in for a look. There are guys there doing building work.

One of them shouts, "Sorry you aren't allowed in here."

I say, "Oh sorry, it's just her first day at this new school in a few days and she hasn't seen in so just wanted her to see it before she starts."

The guy then says, "Aw I went to this primary school. Come with me and we can take a walk around and you can have a look in the windows." Rosie is totally up for it. I can see her wee mind racing taking it all in. She asks a constant stream of questions that I can't answer because the school wouldn't even let me visit because of Covid rules. She's all set with all her uniform ready and she's super excited. The first morning of school she is up and clothes on at six-thirty a.m. I walk her round and come into the playground. I think I am more nervous than her. The PSA is in the playground and comes up straight away to introduce herself to Rosie. Rosie runs off with her and I can see she is asking questions and chatting away. She's got an adult like confidence and assertiveness that is unusual to see in an eight-year-old. I stand awkwardly where the other parents are, they are all in their little groups, obviously all know each other from the years before. A few parents say hello and introduce themselves, which is nice. The teacher then comes out and they all line up. Rosie is in the middle of the line. She doesn't even turn to wave; she's so engrossed in the school environment she isn't even aware that I'm standing there watching. I look on hoping it all goes well...

Annie doesn't start nursery until the end of September so it is just the two of us for a few weeks. It's a luxury to be able to spend the time with Annie on her own and not have to think about responding to two different needs. We go for lots of walks with Angus where we go on bear hunts, coffee shop outings, we spend a lot of time in Asda going shopping. The Asda trips are the most stressful. She wasn't ever really taken out to the shops, so when I do take her, she will just have big meltdowns about wanting to take all the toys home. She really didn't understand the concept at first. There became a lot of rules about coming to the supermarket. She eventually gets used to the rules and the meltdowns are less frequent. I am just happy it is during school hours and it isn't when the shops are really busy. I chose the timing of the shopping and coffee shop visits wisely.

The first nursery visit then comes along quickly. We go for the visit the week before she starts. She keeps saying, "No I'm not going to nursery."

I just keep responding with, "Everyone goes to nursery. Nursery is so much fun."

We park the car just outside the nursery and she says, "No I'm not getting out the car." She won't let me near to unbuckle the car seat.

I say to her "I know it's scary going to a new place and meeting new people but I will be there the whole time."

She then says, "Can we hold hands all the time?"

And I say, "The whole time. I can carry you in if you like."

"Oh, okay then." She happily jumps up in the knowledge that she won't be left alone and this is something we are doing together. We get into the nursery and her key worker comes to meet up, Miss Williams. She's a nice friendly woman who Annie instantly warms to. She gives us a tour and shows Annie where she will hang her jacket and where her tray is and then shows us all the toys inside then takes us outside and shows us the massive play area with bikes and sand and lots of sensory things. Annie looks amazed. She then let's go of my hand and makes a run for the bikes. I take a seat in the play area and just watch her. She comes back and forward. I tell her I won't move from my spot. She's happy about that and then goes away to explore further. After about thirty minutes we need to leave and she says, "Aww I don't want to go."

I'm thrilled by her response. I say, "You are coming back next week and you will have longer to play."

She seems happy about that concept and she happily takes my hand and is okay to leave. It was a successful first visit. I won't lie I was worried in case she had a big meltdown and how I would cope in a nursery full of kids and staff but luckily all was fine.

Chapter 7

Putting in the Boundaries

Today has been a successful day. After continuous escalations in Annie constantly saying no to every little thing that's requested of her – put your shoes on – no. It's time for bed – no. Brush your teeth – no. Leave the park – no – stop your bike – no. And it's not just a no and then a yes, it's a complete meltdown of running away or hitting and kicking and one episode of spitting in my face. We have talked and talked about how we need to be lenient with Annie because it's been a big transition but we also felt that the differing parenting style between us and the foster carer was playing a big part in her behaviour but ultimately, we need to parent the way that fits with us. I bought a little *Peppa Pig* reward chart with Peppa stickers and made a chart of all the tasks she has to do in a day. For every task she does, she gets a Peppa sticker. At the end of the week, she then gets a Peppa prize.

The tasks were simple and all things she can do but was choosing not to when being asked.

1. Get out of bed and put my clothes on.
2. Brush my teeth.

3. Put my shoes and jacket on.
4. Get into my car seat straight away.
5. Get out the car when Mummy tells me.
6. No hitting.
7. No running off, stay close.
8. PJ's on, teeth brushed and up to bed for stories.

Since we have introduced the plan, it's only been two days but oh my God, what a difference in morning routine and bedtime routine. It has been so much easier and actually now enjoyable. I haven't had any big screaming matches or refusals or trying to hit me which has been so much nicer. Instead of dreading it, I look forward to it and feel more in control. Once she gets all her stickers for the week, she then gets a prize. So far, she has fully invested in her plan, let's hope it keeps going in the right direction.

The one thing I didn't think about was how Rosie would respond to Annie getting her *Peppa Pig* chart. So far since being with us Rosie has been challenging in a completely different way to Annie. Rosie doesn't push back with tantrum like behaviour like her sister. She tries her hardest to be super compliant when asked to do something. She has been more challenging because of her constant need for attention, continuous chatter, inability to have quiet time, jealous behaviour when she perceives someone is getting more attention than her and her over-familiarity with strangers, particularly men. I wouldn't use a behaviour chart for these behaviours as she can't really help these behaviours and they are very much a product of her past that wouldn't change from doing a rewards chart.

When we told her about Annie's plan the first thing she said was, "But why don't I have one?." Her question completely took me by surprise but she was absolutely right to ask. She was desperate for a reward chart of her own so she could be reminded how good she was doing. Sometimes it's easy to forget she's just little too and missed out on so many experiences when she was four. She's desperate for praise for everything she does. I went out and bought her a reward chart of her own and she designed it and we came up with tasks that were relevant to her:

1. Say please and thank you.
2. Keep hydrated.
3. Regularly empty my bladder.
4. Get my school clothes ready.
5. Get my clothes for clubs ready and attend clubs (brownies/musical theatre/swimming).
6. Brush my teeth for two minutes (morning and night).
7. No backchat (she came up with that one).
8. No mucking around at bedtime.

Annie is on day four and Rosie is on day two of their plans and I have to say it has been a great thing to do. Since she has come to stay with us, Rosie barely goes to the bathroom, I don't know if it's a fear of missing out or her brain isn't telling her she needs the toilet but she hardly goes to the toilet during the day and was arguing saying she didn't need to go every time we would prompt her to go, which has led to accidents. Today she has been a dream, every time I asked her to go to the toilet, she went happily without any big prolonged discussions around it.

Chapter 8

My Heart Melted

Today I invited my neighbour Emily and her two-year-old son Marcus over for a play date whilst Rosie was at musical theatre. I think I was just as excited as Annie. I had only really known Emily to say hello to before the girls arrived.

When I had Annie out on her bike practising in the street Emily was walking by with Marcus in his pram and Annie cycled up to her and said, "Do you like my bike?"

And from then we exchanged numbers and our friendship blossomed. It was nice to have another mum so close who was also not going out to work and in the mum role 24/7.

Annie was so excited for Marcus to be coming to her house.

She kept saying, "Can I show Marcus my bedroom and my toys and my trampoline?."

I replied, "Yes you can show him everything. It's your house."

She would say, "Is it not your house, it's now my house?"

And I would say, "It's our house and this is where we all live together." She looks at me with unsure, suspicious eyes. It's like she doesn't really believe this is her house and she's going to get to stay here forever.

The doorbell rang and Annie ran to the front door. "Marcus is here, Marcus is here."

She was beyond excited. She was in her element showing Marcus her bedroom and her toys and her trampoline. There was a really special moment when Annie was jumping up and down on the trampoline and she was talking to Emily through the trampoline net. She said, "You're Marcus' mummy and that's my mummy," pointing at me.

Emily said, "Yes that's right, what a clever girl you are."

My heart melted. The rational part of my brain keeps saying it doesn't matter what they call you, you just need to be doing the role. But to hear those words really made me realise how much I am actually craving the label. Because of Rosie's age and the girls were still having contact with birth mum, we didn't introduce ourselves as mummy and mummy in our introduction books. We decided to wait for the time to be right for them to call us mummy. On hindsight, I wish we had just signed it Mummy Nell and Mummy Kit as I think it would have been less confusing for Annie.

Sometimes she would say comments like, "I don't have a mummy."

Or, "I had a mummy that wore a white T-shirt when I was a baby." She doesn't have any memory of living with her birth mum. All she knows is her life when in foster care. We spent so much time planning what would be best to do for Rosie because she was older with more understanding of what was going on that we didn't really anticipate it would be more confusing for Annie and the reality was that Rosie was so desperate to be claimed and be part of a family that she really wanted to call us mummy. So, we could have saved a lot of confusion if we had just started off that way. Hindsight is a wonderful thing.

Chapter 9

Barbie Girl-Crazy Mum

I pick Rosie up from school. She's been in school for a good few weeks now.

She comes running out and I hear a little boy shouting to her, "I'm going to tell your mum you said I could take your clothes off." He's right cheeky looking. There's another little boy laughing behind him. I'm instantly enraged that he thinks he can shout that when I'm standing here. I am thinking *What the hell is going on?* Rosie doesn't seem to be one bit bothered by the comments.

We start walking home and I say, "Why was that boy making those comments?."

"What comments?" she says.

I say, "About you taking your clothes off."

She says, "Aww that's because I was singing the barbie girl song to the boys and it says, 'You can brush my hair, undress me everywhere.'"

I say, "I don't think you should be singing that song, it's not appropriate, especially when the boys are then shouting things like that to you."

"Oh," she replies.

I say, "You shouldn't be singing any songs or making any comments about undressing. You are eight years old." If you sing that song then you need to change the words to 'You can brush my hair and take me everywhere.'"
She says, "But that's not the words."
I say, "I don't care, if you decide to sing it then that's what you have to say."
She looks up at me and says, "Okay Mum."

I walk round to pick her up the following day. She comes running out quite happy.

The little boy that was laughing at the other boy when he was shouting yesterday was walking beside Rosie and he said, "You're lucky you have someone picking you up."

I instantly see red, assuming this is off the back of what comments were made yesterday. I say to him, "Why's that son?" in my most aggressive Glaswegian accent.

He replies in a sheepish voice, "'Cause I don't have someone coming to pick me up."

I stop in my tracks. I don't even have a response. I feel awful. I have completed misread this scenario. All this kid was doing was trying to tell Rosie she was lucky and I'm assuming he's threatening her. What on earth has got into me? I'm suddenly aware of my stress and anxiety levels feeling high which is obviously why I'm acting like a crazy woman. Rosie walks a bit ahead and talks to the little boy as he's walking our way. I don't say anything else. I just walk quietly behind. I feel too guilty and a bit silly for my overreaction. I have a quiet word with myself—I really need to chill.

Chapter 10

The Highs and the Lows

This morning didn't start so well. I just woke up on the wrong side of the bed, even though I had a long lie-in! I just felt moody. I got up and ready and slowly lost my bear with a sore head demeanour. It's Saturday and we have a play date organised to go to the adventure park with one of the neighbours and their daughter, Sylvia. Rosie and Sylvia are similar age and Sylvia was the first play date Rosie has had in her new house. She just lives a few doors down from us. Both Rosie and Annie were both brilliantly behaved. I had a really proud moment when a little girl hurt herself and Rosie came running to me to get help to find her parent. Rosie then remembered what the little girl's dog looked like and went to find her dad. She was so kind and all she wanted to do was help the little girl and make it better for her. For a little girl who has been through so much she is still really kind to others.

After the visit to the park, we decided to have a BBQ since the weather was nice. It was the best decision we could have made. The girls were just beside themselves to be having a BBQ, eating outside and then getting to roast marshmallows on the chiminea. We then sat round the chimenea and told stories. Seeing how happy they were made all the stress of it just so worth it. We were all relaxed and laughing and enjoying each other's company. They both love family time and crave it all the time. I hope that is something that they never loose. When I think into the future, I see us all round the chimenea and laughing and sharing memories of the years we will spend together. It fills my heart.

Sunday could not have been any more different from Saturday. It was a really weird day. It started off so well. We took the girls to Kit's Mum's for a visit and they behaved really well. It has been a work in progress taking Rosie to different places to meet people. She doesn't cope particularly well and gets more and more hyper and then will start to make inappropriate comments that can make people feel uncomfortable, particularly when Annie is getting attention. We have been working really hard on explaining what is acceptable and socially appropriate and she has been taking the advice on board and being much better. After we left Granny's, we went to the big park close by. The girls were playing with a little boy, who was about ages with Annie. Rosie was trying to tell them what to do and play her game.

I could hear the little boy being really quite assertive with Rosie, "No I'm not doing that." As she was trying to boss them into playing tag. The little boy was more interested in just playing around in the sand with Annie. I then sat watching in disbelief as Rosie took herself over to the little boy's Mum and said, "Excuse me, please take your little boy. I don't want to play with him. I just want to be alone with my sister."

The woman just looked at Rosie, astounded. I felt the embarrassment rise right through my whole body. Annie was really quite happy playing with the little boy. I called Rosie over and told her not to go over to the boy's Mum and say things like that.

She said, "But I don't want to play with him and I don't want him near my sister."

I replied, "You can't decide that, if Annie wants to play with him she is allowed to do that." It all appeared to be getting a bit too much for her and we were embarrassed and not completely sure how to manage the situation so we decided to leave. We got stuck in horrendous traffic on the way back home which of course exacerbated Rosie's behaviour. She could not stop speaking. It was excessive, somethings didn't even make sense. It was like she just had to produce sounds from her mouth. Something really triggered her with the little boy or it might even have come before that (we just don't know). For the rest of the day, she was hyper, constant nonsense chatter and regressed back to a three to four-year-old.

As soon as we got into the house she kept saying, "We are having sister time just us alone in my bedroom." If I'm honest I was glad; I really needed a break from listening to her. She took Annie up to her room and of course within five minutes was screaming and balling because Annie was messing her things up. I felt absolutely frazzled. I couldn't comprehend what was going on and I couldn't get a moment to think due to the insistent chatter.

When she came back downstairs and sat to have her dinner she kept saying, "I'm a baby, I'm a baby, I'm a baby," on repeat and other silly things that didn't quite make sense.

I decided to ignore it (maybe the wrong thing to do). She then gets up and started running round the table and trying to get Annie to join in. I took her aside and asked her to calm down but there's just no telling her. It's like someone else has taken over her body. Getting her on her iPad with headphones on seems to be the only thing that gets her back to a semi-relaxed state so that's the strategy I used. I'm not convinced that's the best thing to do. That's what the foster carer told us she did. I was honestly feeling like I couldn't even produce one clear thought. I find it really tough as her behaviour really does have such an influence on Annie and Annie thinks it's 'normal' to be behaving that way. I'm hopeful that the more she settles the less of these behaviours we will see. Sure enough, after spending time on her iPad, she is then more settled and she has her bath and goes to bed. I'm so ready for my own bed.

Monday morning started well until I told Rosie to go upstairs and put tights on as it's too cold for small socks and a summer dress today. You would have thought I told her to go upstairs and put a banana costume on by the way she was acting. I then get them into the car for drop-off (the most stressful part of my day). Annie by the way is doing much better now that she's doing her chart. Rosie sees a little headband that I bought Annie when we went and bought her a new coat and welly boots.

"Why does she get that? I don't have one."

"It's a headband that cost 50p when she got her new coat."

"It's not fair," she replies.

I say, "Rosie when you got your new jacket you got a new bow for your hair that was £5. She isn't getting anything more than you."

She says, "But I want a headband." I think no matter what I said it wasn't going to work. She is hell-bent on the idea that Annie gets more. The car journey then consisted of Rosie trying to wind her sister up to get a reaction the whole way to nursery. Thankfully, distraction is a wonderful thing with a three-year-old. When we get into the nursery playground, Rosie then starts really upping it and running round chasing Annie, similar to the running around the dinner table incident. I feel my anxiety rising. Several times I tell her to stop, but she's not in the head space to listen.

When Miss Sing started walking towards the gate for Annie, Rosie starts shouting really loudly on repeat, "You need to give me a hug, will you miss me?" Annie sees this as a game and starts running riot. I eventually had to guide Annie into the garden holding her hands in between my legs for Miss Sing to close the gate whilst trying to ignore Rosie. I feel other parents watching me, some judging and some probably feeling sorry for me.

We get back in the car and I lose it with Rosie. I'm not proud of the way I dealt with this but I was just at the end of my tether. She then refused to talk to me. The whole journey to school was silent. If I'm honest I was really glad for the quiet. It never happens with Rosie. She then ran straight into school without a goodbye. It left me feeling rubbish all day. What could I have done better, how can I make sure she knows they are equal—all these thoughts whizzing through my mind for the rest of the day. My mind is constantly consumed by these kinds of thoughts these days.

Rosie gets in from school and of course for her, it's all forgotten from her part.

"Can we go to the park?" she asked.

"Firstly, we need to chat Rosie. This morning at the nursery cannot happen again. I understand you were feeling upset but you cannot then run around like that at a nursery drop-off. The nursery staff might say I can't bring you if you continue to do that" (not sure that's what I should have said but I went with it). This grabs her attention.

She says, "Oh I want to come to drop-off." She's now more in the mood for listening.

I say, "You need to learn to contain yourself when that urge comes. I think you do it when you feel a little bit threatened or jealous."

She replies, "I was jealous of Annie."

I say, "That's very honest and mature of you to know that's what it is. The next time I see you getting annoyed because of jealousy I am going to name it and give you a reminder; it's okay to feel that way but it's not okay to run around."

She replies, "Okay, good idea." We then go to the park.

There's definitely more to it that jealously with Rosie, but there's so many little complexities with her that I couldn't possibly unpick every little thing. I also think a big reason for her being unsettled and on edge is not knowing what's happening with contact with her birth mum. I think this has been really confusing for her. The worst bit is that I know more things are coming her way that are going to add to her unsettledness and the worst part is, I am completely powerless to do anything about it. I can't protect her from the news that's about to come. The system has failed these girls time and time again. The social work report that was submitted to the children's hearing system recommended adoption and no further direct contact with their birth mum apart from yearly letterbox contact. Rosie was told this would be happening and had her final contact with her birth mum whilst still in foster care. The week before the girls were moving in with us, there was a children's hearing and one member of the children's panel disagreed with the social work recommendations and argued that the girls should still have direct contact with their birth mum. It was unbelievable. This meant, three weeks after the girls moved in with us, they had a virtual contact with their birth mum.

Rosie at first didn't want to do the call and was saying, "Why am I not being allowed to settle into my new home?"

She was eventually convinced to do the call. It was a really weird experience for me. I was in the kitchen when the social worker started the call. Rosie then automatically turned into what looked like a happy girl. I could hear her saying, "Mummy, Mummy, Mummy," when her birth mum first came up on the screen and sounded excited.

Annie then copied Rosie and started to excitedly shout, "Mummy."

I thought to myself, oh, maybe she felt she wasn't allowed to be excited about it in front of us and I felt sad for her. I wanted to give them space to chat without thinking I was listening so I busied myself and went outside and started to cut the grass to give them privacy so Rosie didn't feel awkward. The social worker then came outside with the laptop and the girls started jumping on the trampoline. I watched for a few minutes then went to the front of the garden to cut the grass. A few minutes later, Annie came looking for me and then a few minutes after that Ruth popped round to say the call was finished.

She said, "Michelle was asking questions about school and things but Rosie wasn't really engaging in the conversation. She was struggling with being asked questions and Annie just wanted to come and find you." I wondered what was going through Rosie's head. Why had that call been difficult for her? What Rosie doesn't know is that Michelle her birth mum is expecting another baby and is due next month. Social workers have told me that once the baby is born then the girls will be told about the baby. I can only imagine how crushing this news will be for Rosie.

Annie doesn't really understand. She thinks Michelle is a woman called Mummy who wears a white top. The takeaway message for Rosie is likely going to be *you have worked hard to keep this baby but you couldn't work hard enough for me.* My heart honestly stops when I think of the hurt and pain she's going to feel.

It pains me to think if the panel members had just listened to the social work recommendations, they would have done their final contact when in foster care and have moved on to their forever family without this hanging over them. Social workers are going to drop this bomb and then arrange another contact with Michelle; I just have no idea how this is going to play out. It's always at the back of my mind just now.

Chapter 11

Peppa Pig is a Success

Anyone who says reward charts don't work have never consistently done them. The *Peppa Pig* chart has been the best thing we have done with Annie. I think part of our success has been:
1. The chart design—Annie loves Peppa and she loves stickers.
2. The chart is colourful and sparkly.
3. She loves that is has been displayed on the whiteboard for everyone to see in the kitchen.
4. It has been an exciting thing to do together at the dining table before she goes up to bed.

On the last day of the week, she lost a sticker for running off at nursery and not waiting for the teacher. I told her this at the dining table and she nearly went into a full-blown meltdown but I quickly let her know that we would put the sticker on and in the morning, she would get one part of her prize then after nursery when she has shown she can wait for Miss Sing before running into nursery she will then get the other part of her prize after nursery. She was eventually accepting of this plan and eager to show she could do it to get the full prize.

When I dropped her off at nursery this morning she was as good as gold. She was delighted to get the first part of her prize which was a *Peppa Pig* book with little *Peppa & George* figures. She hugged me and Rosie and walked nicely through the gate to Miss Sing and the other kids that were being dropped off. She looks so tiny and cute with her little backpack on. She stood right by Miss Sing's leg and gave me a thumbs up. Honestly my heart could melt. She is so cute sometimes. I feel proud of her and I'm also feeling proud of myself too. It's a nice feeling to see there's a change.

It's been interesting watching her respond during the week while doing her chart. There were times where I would say, "Please come and get your PJ's on and teeth brushed."

She would reply, "What will happen if I don't?"

And I would say, "You won't get your sticker and I will be sad because I really want you to make the right choice to get your sticker then you get your prize."

And of course, she would say, "Oh I was just doing something then I'm just coming." As she has a big smile on her face.

"Let's go, it's time for nursery. Shoes and jacket on please."

She replies, "What will happen if I don't?"

"I'm not sure you want to make the choice not to do it. Then you don't get your sticker which means it will take longer to get your prize."

And of course, her response is, "Oh I'm just doing it now."

She's a smart cookie and absolutely knows how to behave. She just needs to get used to it.

I've learned that everything takes double the amount of time with a three-year-old. We didn't have the chance or the time to learn this in advance. People have babies and they literally spend every minute with them as they grow from these tiny little people that can't hold up their own heads or feed themselves and they are completely in tune with their kids and the changes and they adapt right from the birth and they become tuned to the time that they need and take. Having missed out that whole initial stage made my first initial stage with a three-year-old harder to get used to. Now that I'm finally getting used to the change of pace, life is becoming a little bit easier.

Chapter 12

Annie's Fourth Birthday

After a whole lot of debating, will we, won't we have a party. Will it be too much for them to cope with? Will Rosie cope, is it the right thing to do? So many questions, we have only had them for 9 weeks, but, in the end, we decided to have a fourth birthday party for Annie. We invited our family and a few friends over to have a party in the garden. The weather was still warm enough which makes it easier. We played lots of party games and my mum's neighbour made an amazing rainbow cake which Annie just absolutely loved. Thankfully, we had no meltdowns on the day. Rosie coped really well too. We had lots of preparation chats in advance, which definitely helped. We also gave Rosie set tasks that she got to do like make up the party bags, buy a little gift for Annie and wrap it up. They ate so many sweeties and chocolate and cake. When the party finished, Rosie complained of a sore tummy. I thought it was just a bit sore because she had a lot of sugar which she hasn't really had since being with us. When she went upstairs to get her PJs on she projectile vomited all over her bed and then ran to the bathroom and was sick in the sink too which then got blocked! There was a whole family of gummy bears in the sink that hadn't even been chewed!

The first thing she said was, "Can you take a photo so I can show Nana?" I laughed at first and then I couldn't believe I was actually taking a photo so I could show my mum, who had only just gone out for a walk with the dogs. My mum's face was a picture when she came back and I showed her the photos.

This is when I first realised food has been an issue for Rosie. I hadn't really watched how much she ate at the party but my mum and Kit noticed she was eating constantly, which most kids do, but it was excessive. Since she has come here, she has cleaned her plate every mealtime and ate every snack offered. I don't know if she has had periods of time when she has been hungry or meals haven't been consistent but whatever has happened in her past has definitely impacted her relationship with food. I'm not sure she knows when she feels hungry or if she keeps eating because she feels the need to store. It's something I need to keep an eye on.

Chapter 13

Contact with Birth Mum

Contact with their birth mum is scheduled for today. We spoke to Rosie about it last night. She said she didn't want to do it and would only have contact if it was going to be in person. So, I contacted social work to ask about it being face-to-face. I'm feeling anxious about it. I know their birth mum gave birth to a baby boy a few weeks ago and there has been health complications. I don't know if their birth mum will tell the girls herself when she sees them.

Social work arranged for face-to-face contact to happen on Friday afternoon.

I told Rosie the arrangements had been made and her immediate response was, "No I'm not going. I'm not doing it."

I said, "Rosie, social work has arranged this so you don't have to do virtual contact which you said you don't like."

She shouted, "I don't want to; I can't miss my drama class."

I responded, "Don't worry you are allowed to miss your class for special reasons. Your social worker is going to be there. I will take you and be close by and it doesn't have to be for very long."

She replies, "How long do I need to be in the car, I'm not going if I have to ride in the car for long."

I reply, "We have arranged for it to happen closer so we won't be any longer than one hour in the car. I know it worries you but I will be right there."

She looks up with her big brown eyes and says, "Okay I'm only doing it if I can take things with me in the car to do and we can come straight home."

I reply, "Yes of course we can do that."

I check in with her the next day and asked if she wants to chat about it but she very quickly dismisses it. The next day in school when I go to pick her up her teacher asked me to stay behind for a chat. That dreaded feeling I get when I get asked to talk came creeping back up my stomach.

Miss Wilson says, "Rosie has been struggling to manage in the class over the last few days. She has needed a lot of support and redirection. She has been hugging staff and other pupils a lot. I've had to take her aside and remind her that some people don't want to be hugged and she needs to respect personal space." Miss Wilson is a nice kind lady and has a great deal of patience with Rosie. I can see why Rosie likes her. She's firm but fair.

She said, "Rosie has been calling me Mummy today but I have just ignored it and moved on with the rest of the class. I understand she's looking to be claimed at the moment so I'm not making too big a deal about it. But I'm trying to be very clear on boundaries. I have to constantly remind her that I'm the teacher and she's the child."

I reply, "Yes, we are constantly having to do that in the house too. She's like a little Mother Hen to Annie so struggles when we are doing things for her at home."

She ends by saying, "We know the next few weeks will be a struggle but we are prepared to support her through the highs." I thank Miss Wilson and shout for Rosie to tell her we are going home. I feel helpless in that I don't know how to help her through this part. I feel guilty that I felt embarrassed when Miss Wilson told me she was calling her mummy. I didn't anticipate we would go through this kind of thing with Rosie, given she's eight, I assumed she has a much clearer understanding of who everyone is and what their role is. At this point, Rosie was still calling Kit and I by our first names.

It was refreshing speaking with Miss Wilson. Many schools and teachers go on like they are trauma-informed in their practice but I haven't had much positive experience of this being the case, but Miss Wilson's patience and understanding of Rosie's behaviours was really reassuring.

Kit picked Rosie up from brownies later that same night. She was quiet on the way home, which is very unusual because she normally doesn't stop for a breath.

Kit said, "How are you doing, are you feeling okay?" Rosie gave a thumbs down sign.

She said, "I don't want to see my mum on Friday. I just don't want to go. Annie can go but I don't want to.

I've had butterflies in my tummy since you told me I had to do it."

Kit said, "You don't have to do anything you don't want to do. I'm so glad you have told me how feel. We would never want you to have all these worries and feel you have to keep them to yourself."

Rosie went on, "The last time I had to have contact with my mum, I had nightmares for weeks after it."

Kit replied, "Oh darling girl, we just want you to be happy."

Rosie came bounding into the house and ran straight into my arms wanting hugs. Kit then relayed back what she had said in the car. "Oh darling, I'm so sorry you have been feeling like that. We won't ever make you do anything you don't want to do. We never want you to feel like you can't tell us your worries."

She says, "I was nervous to tell you, my tummy has been hurting since Monday."

I just held her in my arms and it took everything in me to not burst into tears. My poor girl has the world on her shoulders. I can't even imagine how she is processing all these feelings in her head. I just want to make it all go away and make it better for her.

She says, "Can we get a worry monster like we have in school and use it for our family?"

I say, "Of course, that's a great idea."

Her enthusiasm for life and excitement for the small things always makes me smile. Even after everything she has been through, she is always, always a glass half-full girl. I just love that about her. I have no idea what the nightmares are about. I know from the reports that there were concerns about unsafe people being in the flat and lots of domestic violence, it could be that. I don't like to pry for information. I will let her tell me when and if she wants.

The next day is Annie's actual birthday and oh my God Rosie was as high as a kite since six-thirty a.m. She had a few presents to open that she didn't get at her party. Rosie would have been sitting on Annie's head if we had let her. She was frantic and continuously talking loudly. Every little parcel Annie opened, Rosie was right beside her trying to rip it open too. We had to ask Rosie to move onto the other couch to give Annie space. She really struggles with Annie getting any attention. When I collected them both from nursery and school, I gave them the option to go to Argos to spent their £15 voucher that they both had from a new home present they hadn't spent yet. I thought it would be good idea so that they were both spending money and getting something. Annie picked two toys straight away and Rosie took ages deciding. She was getting so stressed out by all the options that she started crying. It was just so overwhelming for her. With help, she then chose a blow-up chair and an arts and crafts make-your-own jewellery box set. When we got home, she asked me to blow up her chair. When she took it out the bag she realised it was tiny and more for someone Annie's age or younger. I very unhelpfully got the giggles as soon as I saw it was so small but Rosie on the other hand did not see the funny side and she stormed off in a mood and went to her bedroom. After about ten minutes I followed her upstairs.

She said, "My toys were rubbish and Annie got good toys."

I say, "Your jewellery box is lovely."

She responded, "I want to see my mum now and then I will get good presents." Her comment stunned me into silence.. I wasn't really sure how to respond.

She then said, "Is Annie seeing her?"

I said, "Social work are arranging for Annie to do a short video call on Friday morning."

Rosie responded angrily, "No, no, it has to be in person and I want to go now."

I said, "Okay, okay. I will tell social work and see what they say."

I then just left the conversation there. It's quite a powerless position to be in when I have to listen to her make these requests and then say I need to go and ask social work. I've found that aspect of things difficult. She didn't spend much longer up in her room. She was straight back downstairs trying her hardest to wind up her sister. She was as high as a kite right up until fifteen minutes before bedtime. I had to eventually separate them as I could see how much her hyperactivity was impacting Annie, who was already lacking in sleep and being so grouchy anyway, to then add an overbearing hyper big sister to the mix was just utter chaos! Safe to say it wasn't easy getting Annie upstairs into her bed that night, no matter how much I tried to convince her that she wanted her Peppa Sticker.

The next morning was hard. Seeing Rosie all out of sorts it just painful to watch. She had been scratching her hands during the night and they were all sore. She just isn't able to relax at all. Her wee mind must be racing constantly.

I asked her before I dropped her off at school, "Just so I know what I'm saying when I speak to the social worker… you now want to see your mum in person and don't want to do virtual calls?"

"Yes."

"And if social work asks me why you have changed your mind, is there anything you want me to tell her?"

"I just want presents," in an exasperated voice.

"Okay darling, I will pass it on." We got out the car and she was desperate to run away from me again.

She said, "I want to punch you and that car."

I replied, "I know you have a lot going on just now but there will be other ways that might ease the load rather than punching me or a car."

"Yes, I will run, I don't want to walk with you. Go away."

"I will stand here and watch until you have reached the gate safely"

"Why?"

"Because you are stuck with me for the rest of your life now, and I want to make sure you get to school safely."

"You're disgusting, bye," as she runs off without looking back.

"Bye, have a good day." Waving and smiling but on the inside, I just want to scream. Longing for the day that these interactions don't happen and we just have normal ordinary parent-child interactions.

It's hard to not listen to the things she is saying. The rational part of my brain completely understands why but the human more emotional part of me craves the time where she will say, 'I love you, bye Mum' and hopefully mean it. Until that time comes (it might never come) I will keep plodding along trying to do and say the right thing. Which I know I don't always do. But I am learning, we are only human. Every day is a school day with these girls and I need to give myself a break.

Of course, I then get in late from dropping Rosie off and then I can't get connected to the bloody laptop and I'm twenty minutes late for the virtual meeting with social work. These social workers are nice people. I really don't have anything against them but my God I can't wait to get my life back where I don't need to schedule visits or meetings or phone calls and just get on like a normal family. After much debate, it was agreed that Ruth, the girls social worker would collect presents from Michelle, the girls birth mum and bring them to Rosie and Annie will do a ten-minute virtual call when at nursery. Then Ruth also told me that she would be telling Rosie about her new brother when she comes. My heart sank. I have no idea how this is going to play out but I'm thinking the best thing I can do is predict, plan and prepare.

Chapter 14

The Dreaded Day…

It's Friday. Ruth arrived about ten-thirty a.m. I have this feeling of dread. She's a nice lady, and has been a good social worker to the girls but I just want this part of my life to be done. We drive together to Annie's nursery where its arranged that Annie will do the virtual call with her birth mum in a room in her nursery. We get put into the office space. Everything about it feels weird. Her little face when she comes running into the room confused, and not leaving through the normal gate that all the other kids use just made my heart so sad. I stay in the room when the call starts. I don't think about whether I should be there or not, but I just want to be close for her, plus my meeting with Michelle had previously gone so well so I thought it wouldn't do any harm. Although Annie doesn't understand it all, she's always unsettled when Ruth visits. The video call cuts off after a few minutes and Ruth asks me to wait outside. I am confused but leave straight away as requested. It just feels like it was made to be awkward and it didn't have to be. I honestly feel so removed. Why couldn't I have just stayed? I walk to outside the nursery building. I get my phone out and text Kit saying I'm outside as Annie's in there with Ruth on the video call. She asked me to leave the room. I'm like the spare prick at the party. After a few minutes Annie comes running out to me with her arms spread out and jumps up with a big smile on her face. My heart aches. Ruth followed saying, "She was just wondering where you were after you left so I had to stop the call."

I thought to myself *Maybe if you hadn't awkwardly put me out the room then it might have gone better.* I don't say anything. We get back in the car to go back to the house. On the drive, Annie is the quietest she's been since being with us. She must get so confused. She has this little worried look on her face. I can only imagine she is wondering if she is moving somewhere different, where and who will she be with next. I just try to reassure her as much as I can. It must be as so hard for her to comprehend everything that is going on.

We get back to the house and Annie stays in the house with Kit and Ruth and I walk over to the school to collect Rosie. She is quite happy to see me, obviously forgetting that she thought I was disgusting this morning. We walk home hand in hand as she sings a line from a song in a movie she's been watching on repeat, *Someday it's going to be ordinary, someday it's going to be extraordinary.* My heart aches for her. The lines of that song have so much meaning for us. We have all been striving for 'normal' since we were matched as a family. She really is an extraordinary little girl. She has no idea the news Ruth is going to share with her is going to be one of the worst days in her life and a day she will never forget. My anxiety is through the roof.

We get back home and after a bit of chat in the living room, Ruth takes Rosie to the dining table to chat and I play doctors with Annie in the front room. Kit goes back upstairs to her office because she is working. I can't believe I am able to put my game face on and play the role of an Aussie doctor pretending to fix Annie's bottom, foot and pinkie toe after a pretend fall from a trampoline. I am so anxious on the inside.

As I am examining Annie's toe Ruth pops her head in the front room, "Nell can I speak with you for a second?."

I will never forget the expression on her face. I just know it hasn't gone down well.

She says, "I've told Rosie about the baby and she has locked herself in the downstairs toilet." Ruth tries to speak to Rosie from outside the door.

"Rosie, I know you are upset and you might not want to speak. Can you knock once to let me know you are okay." Silence. "Can you knock to let me know you have heard me?" A little knock comes from the door. I get a knife and I open the lock from the outside.

I say, "Hi Rosie, it's me. I know Ruth has just told you about the baby. I'm so sorry this is happening; I can't imagine how you are feeling darling. I know you might want some time on your own, but you don't have to sit in there. You can go to your room or if you need me I can come in?" A little knock comes from the door. "Knock if you would like me to come in." I say. I hear a little knock. I open the door and she falls into my arms. She is just sobbing so hard.

I hold her so tight and I keep saying, "I'm so sorry darling. There's nothing about this that is fair. Do you want to go upstairs or do you want to have a cuddle on the sofa?"

"Sofa," she replied through a snotty nose. I just sit with my arms wrapped around her. What can I even say that will make her feel better? We just sit for ages in silence as she sobs. . Ruth then takes over playing doctors with Annie, I doubt her Aussie accent is as good as mine. After about ten minutes Rosie says , "Can I go to my room and go on my iPad? I don't want to speak to Ruth anymore?."

"Of course, you can, I will explain to Ruth."

Poor Ruth looks so drained. I actually feel sorry for her. I know if she had it her way that Rosie would have not found out this way. They had wanted Michelle to tell the girls before their final contact. She has a long drive home back up north and its already nearly five p.m..

We decide to take the girls to McDonald's for an ice cream sundae after dinner. I don't think any of us really know how to act or what to say. Rosie is a million miles an hour, where she does this thing where she constantly talks but doesn't really make much sense or have a two-way conversation. It's just noise. She doesn't say anything about the news again that night. It probably won't be until she goes to bed that she will let herself quietly think about it.

It's Saturday and I'm going for my first girls' night out since the kids came to live with us. . My best friends from school, Davina, Lizzy and Cat are coming through and we are booked into a hotel in the city and going for dinner and drinks. I'm beyond excited to see them and get out and feel 'normal'. Kit takes the girls to their cousin's sixth birthday party during the day. In the car on the way to the party Rosie says " I took care of Annie all the time when we lived with our birth mum.

She continues , "I had to give her her bottle every night and put her to bed and I had to change her nappy."

Kit doesn't want to get into asking too many questions as Annie is in the car too,. She just allows her to put the statements out there without any follow-up questions.

It's Sunday afternoon and we take the kids for a long walk after they had too many sweets and were really excited after seeing my friends and getting yet more presents. I'm feeling a bit fragile so the fresh air will do me good. Kit is walking behind with Annie and Rosie and I walk hand in hand just ahead.

She says to me, "Did you ever have any other kids before us?" I

Reply "No, I haven't had any other children."

She continues, "Why didn't you decide to be a foster carer?"

I answer, "Because foster carers only get to keep the children they look after for a little while. I wanted children to be part of our family forever."

She thinks for a while then says, "Have you ever changed a baby's nappy?"

I reply, "Yes, I've changed Callie's nappy"

She says, "Have you ever taken care of a baby?"

I say "Yes, when I babysat Callie when she was a tiny baby. Are you asking about this because you are thinking about your brother who has just been born?"

She looks up like she's been caught out. She says, "No. He's not my brother because he doesn't live with me."

I say, "He is biologically your half-brother; you have the same biological mum."

She says, "Why is he living with my mum? How can she take care of a baby when she can't even take care of me and Annie?"

I look down and say, "I don't know darling. I wish I had the answers for you."

She then says, "Why doesn't he come and live with us?"

I think carefully before answering this one and then say, "Because he is staying with your mum."

She butts in, "But Mum can't look after him. I looked after Annie when we lived with her. I changed her nappy, fed her every night and had to do everything. How is she allowed to keep him?."

I say, "I don't know darling. Maybe you should write down a list of questions and ask Ruth when she visits next week?"

She says, "Yes, I want to know why he can't be with me. Can I go and play in the park now?"

I say, "Yeah sure, go on." I just watch as she runs into the play park. On the outside looking in she just looks like any normal happy-go-lucky eight-year-old. It pains me that the reality of it is just so different. It's so unfair that she has all these worries. I just wish I could protect her more from all of this. It's a powerless position to be in as an adoptive mother.

It's Monday morning. I ask her on the walk to school, "Would you like to see a photo of your brother?"

She says, "Yeah okay. And I'm writing my list of questions when I come home."

I reply, "Okay I will ask for a photo today so you can hopefully see one tonight."

Straight after school we go to gymnastics. She's doesn't ask a thing about the photo. I purposefully don't bring it up and wait until after dinner until I have her attention at the dinner table.

I say, "Why don't you get your notebook and start writing down some of your questions?"

She replies, "Yes, I will get my sparkly notebook." She then starts her list. This is what she writes: :

1. Why is my mum getting a second chance when she had two years to fix things and she didn't?

2. Why is my brother getting to stay with my mum and me and Annie can't?

3. Why can't I go back and live with my mum?

She reads her questions out to me and then says, "Is there anything else I should ask?"

I say, "You should ask as many questions as you want darling. You deserve answers. As an adult I'm struggling to understand the decisions that have been made so I can only imagine how important it will be for you to get answers. Ruth sent me some photos of your brother for you. Now your brother is in hospital because he wasn't very well when he was born so he has some tubes that he needs for feeding in the photo."

She looks up, "Will he be okay?"

I say, "Yes, as far as I'm aware he's had all the surgeries he needs to fix him. He just needs to stay in hospital for the nurses and doctors to help him."

I get my phone out and show her the photos. She is so quiet as she scrolls and enlarges each image. I walk round to her side of the table and I can see that she has wet herself.

"Darling, can you go upstairs and have a quick body shower and just put your PJs on."

She says "Why?" Completely unaware.

I say, "You have had an accident."

She looks down and says , "Oh yeah."

She didn't even argue. She looks so small and vulnerable.

She said, "Can you come up and get me a towel and my PJs." I follow her up and gather her things for her. I feel so helpless at times like these. I so badly want to make life better for her and it pains me that I can't fix it and all I can do is ride the storm and hope that she gets through the other side. The worry she must have in her mind about the baby must be so overwhelming, that her physical response is to wet herself and not be aware. I wonder just how much trauma she has been through.

Chapter 15

The Honest Truth

It's been a tough few days for Rosie. She didn't have a great day at school today. They were doing a class project building a castle out of recycling and were asked to partner up and go in small groups. She asked another kid in her class to be partners and she ignored Rosie and asked to join a group with other kids. Rosie then decided to work on her own. Her castle then broke and it was just chaos. The teacher said it was such a build-up and she was already feeling out of sorts because she had been left on her own. The teacher said she manged to calm things down and get her back on track but it sounded like it was the last thing she needed to happen given everything else that's going on for her.

The next morning is heartbreaking. We are Walking along the road to school and there's four of her classmates on the other side of the road waiting to cross at the lollipop man.

She shouts , "Morning, morning, hi guys," and is so enthusiastic... Every single one of them look at her and ignore her. My heart breaks for her. I just can't even imagine how she must feel having to deal with that kind of thing every day. I also completely get it. For other kids it's really hard to be around a kid like Rosie. In their eyes, she is bossy, unable to compromise and uninterested in their ideas. We know she's just a kid that's missed out on so much important interactions and experiences that every other child has been fortunate enough to experience. I just so desperately want them to get past that stuff and see the kind, considerate, patient girl we see, especially when taking care of her sister.

After school and nursery pick up we all go down to the beach for a walk with Angus. . I so desperately need to do something as a four today and have adult company. I actually get jealous of Kit going to work every day. It sounds crazy and I'm surprised I feel that way. I just miss doing something that's for me. I'm so engrained in this caregiver's role that I feel I've lost all my other important roles that give me meaning and purpose: worker, colleague, wife, sports enthusiast, friend, family member. Yesterday I even made the impulsive decision to sign up for the Edinburgh Marathon 2022. After signing up I instantly felt better. This is something I am doing for me. Nothing to do with the adoption, or the girls. It's purely my thing and it feels good. Let's see if I'm saying that when it gets to May next year and I need to run 26.2 miles.

We get back from the beach and we eat our fish and chips and then I sit with Rosie at the table.

I say , "I've spoken to Ruth and shared your concerns/questions. They have explained it as it isn't so black and white that your mum is getting a second chance. Social workers are working really closely with your mum and if anything at all happens or they feel the baby is unsafe he will be taken into care to ensure he's looked after."

"I want him to go into care. I hate my mum," she replies.

"It's okay to feel a whole host of emotions about your mum. There's a lot that's happened in your life that you are allowed to be sad and angry about. It's definitely okay to miss your mum too and I don't ever want you to feel guilty that you would rather be living with your mum. I completely understand. You can still miss her and be mad at her at the same time."

"I don't want to be with her. I hate her. I just want the baby to be okay."

The next bit of the conversation just breaks my heart.

She says, "Do you know why I get sad? Annie is getting so much more than I got when I was four. She's getting play dates and going to clubs and having family time and all I got was locked in the flat looking after her. It's not fair."

I say, "You are right. It isn't fair. You deserve the world and I'm so sorry that has happened to you. I can only tell you now that you are our priority and I want to you experience everything that everyone else has and gets. I want you to think of everything that every other eight-year-old gets and know that you will get that with us."

She says, "Okay. Can we just hug now."

I hug her as tight as I can. In my head I am saying to myself, *Do better tomorrow Nell. She needs so much more than meets the eye. Be better at giving her what she needs tomorrow.*

Chapter 16

Answered Questions

It's been just over a week since Rosie found out about her new sibling. It's Friday and Ruth has come back to visit. I realise only after her visit how uptight I have been about the whole thing. I can't even imagine how Rosie is feeling. Rosie point blank refuses to talk to Ruth.

She says , "I don't want to speak to Ruth. I don't want to speak about any of it I just want to be happy."

I say , "I just want you to be happy too but I also want you to have your questions answered. It's important you get the information that you want and deserve to know."

She says, "You do it for me and tell me. I just don't want to."

I reply, "Please at least say hello to Ruth. Ruth only wants things to be good for you and give you answers."

She says, "I won't be rude. I will say hello and then go on my iPad in my room."

That's exactly what she does.. She isn't rude, or unpleasant. She says hello and requests to leave the room. But I can see in her face how much she desperately doesn't want to be here, in the same space as Ruth.. Her eyes are filling up. She probably associates Ruth with bad news now, so is probably terrified of what answers she will be bringing. Rosie is naturally a pleaser. I can see she desperately wants to be seen as behaving and doing as she is told but her body is edging out of the room without her even being aware of it.

Ruth understands where Rosie is coming from. To be fair even before she found out about her sibling being born, she was already asking when Ruth would stop visiting. Ruth decides to write down answers to Rosie's questions:

1. Why does Mum get a second chance?
   - Your brother is not living with Michelle just now. He is living at hospital as he had to have an operation on his belly. Nurses and doctors are looking after him just now.
   - When you and Annie were living with Michelle, she did not look after you properly. When adults were worried about what you and Annie were going through, you then had a social worker and their job was to make sure you were okay. Your brother has a social worker who sees him and Michelle every day. If there are any worries about Michelle keeping your brother safe, the social worker will help him.

2. Why does my brother get to stay and we don't?
   - Josh is a new baby and Michelle has not looked after him by herself before. He is in

hospital and is being looked after by nurses and doctors just now. We don't know for sure if he will go home long-term.
- When you and Annie lived with Michelle you went through a lot and were not safe. You now have a new home and family who love and care for you and Annie. We don't want you to go back to living with Michelle and go through difficult things again.

Ruth leaves and Kit takes the written questions up to Rosie in her room.

She reads it and then scrunches it up and says, "I don't need this paper any more and I don't have any more questions."

I go up after Kit and say, "You might have questions later once you have digested the information that Ruth has wrote."

"I won't," she snaps. .

And true to her word when I check in with her, and she consistently says, "I don't have anything else to ask."

The next face-to-face contact is supposed to happen on the first Monday of the October break. The whole legal thing is so messy. Every time Rosie refuses to see Michelle then we are technically breaching the legal order from the children's panel. The legal team for social work said that 'unless Rosie is at risk of harm then contact needs to go ahead'. These are the kind of people and comments that have really frustrated me throughout this whole process. These people don't see the child that's struggling in the middle of all their legal decisions. If we look at it from their black and white perspective then yes okay, Rosie isn't at immediate risk from Michelle but if we dive into the big grey area that we call life then there are several risk factors that I can think of:

1. Rosie for the first time in her life has shared that she had nightmares and 'butterflies' in her tummy after the first contact and is clearly demonstrating she has felt comfortable with us to share this information and for us to support and protect her. If we then continue to make her engage in contact then our new relationship is at serious risk when we are trying our hardest to be her trusted adults. How can she trust us if we can't protect her and listen to her needs?

2. We have now seen the different presentations in Rosie's behaviour. When not needing to go to contact or think about any of these things she is much more able to engage in her new relationships, school and club activities. When she is under the threat of contact happening, she is anxious, hyperalert and unable to connect with others. Her brain is so overactive that she can't function the way she so desperately craves. This might not be seen as a risk, but it just seems so unfair on her. Every day I watch her peers reject her, other adults struggle to understand the hyperactivity and knowing if all of this was not taking place then they would be getting to see the

more relaxed, open and likeable girl we know that she is.

3. If we keep putting her through this then we are going to do so much more damage in the long-term. It really is as simple as that. We are trying so hard to calm down her sympathetic nervous system, that 'fight or flight' response and engage her parasympathetic nervous system so she can rest and digest. Every time even the idea or the unknown of what is happening with contact comes up, she gets stuck in the fight or flight. If only these people could understand the long-term damage they are doing by continuing to put her through this. She physically and mentally needs a break. She needs to have the chance to feel safe and secure with no threats to her.

Chapter 17

The Show Must Go On

So, contact is going ahead. Despite my feedback to social work, we are told it has to happen as we are not allowed to breach the legal order. Such a powerless position to be in as adopters. The only thing we can do is pull our big girl pants on and help the girls prepare for it. It's the first day of the October holidays and the contact is happening today. We requested it happen today as it gives Rosie time to digest whilst on holiday so the meeting won't then have an impact on her behaviour in school. Kit drops them at the contact centre and Ruth is supervising it. The girls didn't say much about the contact at all apart from telling us about every sweet they ate. It is strange and surprising but Rosie definitely appears more settled after seeing Michelle in person, which we are both pleased with. Ruth phones me after the contact with Michelle. She tells me "contact was hard for Rosie. Rosie stood at the opposite side of the room for the first while and didn't hug Michelle to begin with, but once Annie was getting lots of attention Rosie then warmed up to getting closer. Michelle had asked Rosie several times if she wanted to keep seeing her and Rosie kept saying 'no' and just looking down. Michelle struggled with Rosie saying no and kept asking. Eventually after being asked several times, Rosie then changed her answer to yes. I honestly don't really know what Rosie is thinking about the whole thing. Ruth told me that they would be requesting another children's hearing and they would be arguing for their original recommendation of letterbox contact to take place over continued face-to-face contact.

We take the girls to my mum's for their first little holiday for the October school break. I am really quite nervous about it but overall, it goes really quite well. Rosie is buzzing. My mum really made a fuss and got her room all made up lovely for her. Annie is a bit more confused and unsure by it all.

She keeps saying, "Is this my new house? Do I live here now?" With lots of reassurance by the end of the three days, she came to understand it wasn't a new house that she was going to be left at and she would be going back to her own house as normal.

It's the end of the holiday break, a letter comes through the post to notify us that the children's hearing is scheduled for the 10th of November 2021. It will be then that they will decide if the girls will continue contact or if it will go back to original social work recommendation of yearly letterbox contact. I'm really worried about the outcome. Rosie is still adamant she doesn't want to continue seeing her mum in person. I'm still unsure of why she feels this way. I think she is scared that Michelle might have some sort of control over whether she stays here or would have to go back. I don't like to pry too much and just let Rosie talk about it when she is ready. My biggest fear is if they force rules on having to have contact I can only imagine it will do more harm than good.

Chapter 18

Inst vs Reality

It's the week before Halloween. We decide to decorate the house with Halloween decorations and carve pumpkins. The Insta post would suggest it was the best night ever. Whereas in reality Rosie's perfectionism and inability to give control of the carving over to the adult made the whole experience a constant argument. I honestly thought *There's no way she's enjoying this.* Once I carved her unicorn in her pumpkin and she got the end result she was absolutely delighted.

"Take a photo of me doing this."

"Take a photo in live mode."

"Make sure you capture the amazing shape."

I was thinking, *Wow maybe this is just the reality for all activities.*

It comes to bedtime and Kit takes Annie up for her stories. I give Rosie the option of chatting with me or going on her iPad. She chooses her iPad so I tidy up, make the packed lunches and put the washing on. I am then getting my waterproofs on to take Angus out for a walk.

The weather is miserable but the poor dog is s cross-legged.

"Rosie it's bedtime. iPad off, brush your teeth please."

"You have to put me to bed," she shouts.

I'm instantly irritated by the demand as I'm half putting my welly boot on.

"No, I will say goodnight here, I need to take the dog out, he's desperate," I reply.

"No, you have to take me upstairs and put me to bed now." The demanding tone really triggers me. I have to say I'm not proud of how I then respond . Her demand that I go up and put her to bed really pushes my buttons. I rip the welly boot off and I fly upstairs so quickly, roughly draw the blind and say e, "Right, are you happy, now get into bed."

Of course, as you can imagine my response does not make her happy or indeed make her get into bed or play ball at all. If I take myself out the emotion of the situation she was really only asking for a bit of nurture before bed.

The night ends with her shouting , "Get out of my room."

There is no nice cuddle or kiss goodnight. Of course, as soon as I leave I take the dog out a walk and feel absolutely awful What on earth possessed me to act that way? Why did it matter how she said it? Why did I not just go upstairs and put her to bed? I'm an absolute monster. She's never going to want to talk to me tomorrow.

I barely sleep a wink replaying the whole thing. Way to go me, I am already feeling exhausted and now it's my very own fault I've added to the exhaustion because I'm now not able to sleep because of the guilt of my own actions.

It's the next morning and I'm expecting a very frosty shoulder from Rosie but what I get is quite the opposite.

"Morning, guess what? Today I'm really excited because I have musical theatre and I get super noodles."

I am gobsmacked. Why on earth doesn't she hate me right now?

I say "I'm really sorry I acted like that last night; I was really tired and felt stressed by trying to get everything done before bed but it wasn't your fault so I'm sorry for acting like that."

"It's fine. Guess what, I'm doing in fun thirty-one in class today...." Unbelievable. I can't believe all is forgiven so quickly.

I still don't like the way I acted. I know it's the demanding tone she used that triggered me but on reflection I know I was being really impatient with Annie too. I feel ashamed that I don't have the patience and compassion that they deserve. . I then go on a bit of a mission to start making sure my own cup is full so I can consistently respond in the best way to the girls. I'm going to try to ensure I go out a walk or a run at least once a day just with the dog, trying to go for a sauna or a swim when I can and also try to see family and friends more and take a bit more time out and to energise. I have also downloaded audible books and started reading *Calm Parents, Happy Kids*. This has been a great reminder of what I need to be working on when interacting with the girls, especially Rosie who requires a great deal of attention. I need to remember not to always be sergeant major all the time and try to be more playful in my interactions.

After a few days of my newfound approach, I'm already seeing such a difference with Annie's compliance when I'm being more playful. For example, tonight I managed to get her to eat her full bowl of lentil soup because I spoke in an Asian accent pretending I wanted the soup for my own tummy and it was devastating every time she took a spoonful of my soup. I need to do more of this, not always with the Asian accent, mind you.

Chapter 19

I'm Drained

I was feeling so rotten last night. Such a headache and upset stomach. I think all the anxiety is really affecting me physically. Waking up early this morning to Annie's knocking was painful. It took everything in me not to be a bear with a sore head. The saving grace was the fact we were meeting Kit's friends and their kids for a playdate in the afternoon but when the dreaded text came to cancel because their kids were ill, I felt my heart sink! How am I going to cope with them all day without any structured activities? They are already arguing and constantly on the wind up! First thought is—I need to tire them out! First thing's first, let's get Annie out on her bike and get the stabilisers off. Nursery staff had said she's already nearly there when on the bikes at nursery so she's definitely ready. And sure enough, one little push, and off she goes. Rosie came out on her roller skates and puts her all into trying to go them. She's much less confident than Annie. Annie doesn't even think about falling whereas Rosie is much more careful. We decide to go to the promenade for the afternoon. Of course, in the car on the way, Rosie is in a moaning mini mood. Anything she could have moaned about she did.

I say , "Rosie why must you moan about everything? Why can't you just enjoy the moment and stop moaning?"

"I can," she replies .

"Well do it then," I say. . Then there's silence in the car. I immediately start to feel guilty. I can see her wee face in the mirror just looking out the window. That guilt is building again. I think to myself *Are we there yet in our parent child relationship? Can I actually make these super direct comments the way I see other mothers speak with their kids?* The answer is I don't know.

We get to the promenade and the whole way to the end she doesn't moan once. Her wee face is concentrating trying to roller skate. I feel bad. The effort she needs to put in roller skating as well was double the work because she walks with them rather than lets her feet roll along the ground, no matter how often I tell her the proper technique and demonstrate , she of course, knows best and is doing it her way. On the way back we hold hands and chat. Poor Kit got the short straw dealing with Annie whose favourite word again at the moment is no.

Rosie says to me, "Can you tell me everything about Christmas and what we will be doing?" I do my best to explain what Christmas morning will look like and what we have for Christmas dinner and going to the panto on Christmas Eve and the Christmas dinner party we host with our friends and their kids.

She says , "Tell me in more detail though."

I say , "I don't know what more detail you want. Why don't you ask me detailed questions and I will give detailed answers?"

"No, I just want to know more." It is actually such a lovely conversation. She's really quite settled here and it's so heartwarming to hear how excited and curious she is about future events as part of this family.

Annie is definitely not as settled as Rosie at the moment. They like to take turns.

Tonight, I take her up to bed, we read some stories and the last story I say , "Can I sit on your bed?"

She says , "You can come and lie down." I lay down beside her in the bed and read her *Peter Rabbit*.

After the book is finished, I say , "Do you want to cuddle?"

She says , "Yes, good idea."

I then cuddle into her and within a minute she says , "Okay goodbye." It's tough knowing that my presence isn't a comfort for her yet and she would rather be on her own going to bed.

Chapter 20

The Impact of the Children's Hearing

The children's hearing is supposed to happen tomorrow, Tuesday. I get an email tonight to say that it's very likely it will be deferred due to an error the children's reporter has made with documents being sent out to the wrong address. They sent out our documents to Michelle by accident which has our surname and address. We were told they were retrieved before they got opened but due to Michelle not receiving her letters on-time they said it had to be fair and her solicitor needed time to read the reports fully before the hearing. The dread I feel in my body just thinking about telling Rosie that it isn't going ahead as planned is crippling. I pick her up from school and she is super hyper. As we walk round to the house, I tell her the hearing has been cancelled and will now be taking place in two weeks' time.

She immediately goes quiet and says, "Can I have sweeties?"

I say, "No you need to go and take your uniform off and get ready for cheerleading." "Why, it's so unfair!" she shouts. She runs upstairs and starts to cry. I know it isn't about the sweeties. She has been desperate for this hearing to happen and 'just get on with her new life' as she puts it. I leave her for ten minutes then she comes down to the kitchen.

"I know it's frustrating and I know you just want clarity and to move forward. But it's out of our control at the moment."

"I know. Can I have a sweetie now?"

"Yes, you can." Her trick or treat Halloween bucket is still overflowing. "Take three," I say.

Like the timing couldn't get any worse Ruth is now moving on to a new post and the girls are being allocated a new social worker. They asked to come out to visit the girls today. When I pick Annie up from nursery she is on good form. She is chatting as usual telling me all about her day.

She then says , "You drive like Freda."

Freda is the foster carer that she lived with before coming here.

I say , "Oh do I?"

And she says , "Yes but I don't live with Freda any more. I want to live with her but I know I can't." It honestly feels like I am getting shot right through the heart. "Can I go back to Freda's?." she continues.

"Sorry darling. Freda is just a foster carer. She takes care of children for a short time until they find their forever families. You have found your forever family now so you don't need to be in foster care."

"I want to be," she replies. She then she starts humming and the conversation comes to a close. Before the girls came to live with us, social workers kept preparing us that Annie would settle and attach quicker due to her age and it would take much longer with Rosie. But what we have found is that Rosie has been so vocal about how much she loves us and how much she wants to be here and Annie has pushed back much more. When I shutdown my emotional mind and use my wise mind, I am able to comprehend why. Foster care is all Annie knows. She was also only two years old and treated like a princess by Freda. Rosie was treated well but our experience of being in their company was Annie was favoured over Rosie. Now they are with us we have been very quick to ensure both girls are treated equally. We have also been very quick to set limits and boundaries, especially with Annie who was very demanding and when she didn't get her own way was quite aggressive. We haven't tolerated that behaviour and laid down the law with our house rules from the start, with no real exceptions. We are starting to see a shift in her behaviour in a more positive way which is great but we are hoping the attachment will start to improve in the coming months. She is now more attuned to the response she gets from us and there is an awareness it's different from Freda's.

Chapter 21

Don't Underestimate How Important One-on-One Time Is

Rosie got a really good report from school for parents' consultation. The teacher said that academically Rosie is the top of the class. She is in the top reading, writing and maths group. She does need lots of direction to listen and not talk over people and the teacher but for the majority of the time she is behaving really well and is trying her best. This is major progress. Miss Wilson said she used the calm corner twice this week. Once on Monday and twice on Tuesday.

I said, "it was supposed to be the children's hearing on Tuesday and she has been worrying about it so it's likely she went to the corner due to feeling worried about that."

Miss Wilson said, "Yes I asked if she was okay and she said she was worried but didn't want to talk about it." Miss Wilson said, "She is so resilient. She is enthusiastic about everything we do and despite things being really unsettled for her she is doing a great job to manage." Miss Wilson spoke about how they are supporting her to engage more with peers and how they are managing the over-familiarity with adults. I liked the way they seemed to have a handle on how they were responding. We need to remind ourselves that Rosie pretty much missed out on nursery and primary one and had to repeat primary two. Despite this hard start, she is doing incredibly well. We decide we really want to make a big deal about the good report. We tell her she is going to get a treat for her doing so well at school. She is so excited. She writes a list of things she would like to do and we take some of her suggestions and add our own. We decide I will take her swimming on her own on Saturday morning and then Kit will take her for shopping and lunch in the afternoon. She is beyond excited, until of course she finds out that Annie is getting to go swimming on Friday afternoon.

"Why does she get to go swimming? She hasn't been good?" she shouts.

I reply, "She has been good. We all need to learn, no one is perfect. Plus, it's not about her behaviour. Everyone should get the opportunity to learn to swim."

"But that's not fair. That's my treat." As she stomps her feet and crosses her arms.

I say, "What Annie does has nothing to do with what you will be doing." Her little face is just looking at me furiously, but she stops arguing and disappears to the front room.

Later on, she hears me saying to Annie, "We need to get you football trainers and football top for football training."

I didn't know she was listening until her head pops up from the sofa. "Why does she need that?" she says.

"She's four now so she can go to football training for four to five-year-old age group but she needs proper trainers, she can't go in her *Peppa Pig* slip-ons. Would you like to come with us to help her pick out what she needs?" I reply.

"No, I'm not helping her. I hate her," she says.

"I don't believe you hate your sister Rosie; I think you are feeling a bit jealous."

"I do hate her and I'm not coming," she says as she then retreats back onto the sofa. She stays in the house with Kit and I take Annie to get her kit sorted. When I get back home Kit just gives me the look of 'what a nightmare'. Rosie had been writing notes to Kit saying, *I don't belong in this family.* Kit said she was then saying she wants Annie to go and live somewhere else or she will.

Kit said, "That's not going to happen. You might feel jealous of your sister sometimes but she's your sister and you have always been together."

"She's so annoying I hate her," she says.

"We are all annoying at times, that's what families do," Kit replies.

Later that night when Kit is putting Annie to bed, I say , "Do you want to play a card game?."

"No," she replies.

"Do you want to do anything?" I enquire.

"Not sure," she replies.

I say, "Okay I tell you what, I'm going to talk like I'm you and you interrupt me if what I'm saying is wrong?" She just looks at me with her eyes wide open, intrigued.

I start. "I'm feeling really unsettled and nervous just now. There has been a lot of change and uncertainty in my life that hasn't been fair. Sometimes I feel sad and sometimes I feel happy. Sometimes I like living here and sometimes I don't. Sometimes I miss living at Freda's and sometimes I miss living with my birth mum. Sometimes I feel angry that things couldn't have been better at my birth mum's then I could have stayed there for all of my childhood. I just really want set answers so I know what I'm doing and I can stop getting butterflies in my tummy and so I can relax."

I stop speaking and it is silent. She is fidgeting with a little squishy toy. I am wondering if she has stopped listening. I then continue, "Sometimes my sister really annoys me for legit reasons and sometimes I just feel a bit jealous because I feel like she gets so much more that what I got when I was four." Silence.

She then says without looking up, "I don't feel sad that I'm not with Freda and I do like it here."

I say, "Okay well if there's anything else you want to chat about, I'm here to listen. It's okay that you feel all these different things at different times."

"I know that," she says.

"Good, now let's snuggle on the couch before you have to go to bed?." I nudge her in the direction of the sofa.

We lay there watching some cartoon programme about princesses and she is accepting of cuddles and I play with her hair. It's moments like these I realise she has missed a lot of physical touch and nurture. I think to myself *You need to get better at this Nell* . It's so easy to forget when you are running around having to help her organise everything and be there and do that and split them up because all they do is fight. It's easy to forget that Rosie needs it just as much as Annie. There's that guilt creeping in again. It never goes far.

Saturday morning swimming is a dream. She is just delighted to be by herself for one-on-one time. She is absolutely brilliant when she's on her own and not having to compete with her sister. I actually really enjoy my time with her. She is great company. She loves playing in the water and being with me. The difference going with Rosie compared with Annie is like night and day. Annie is desperate to go off on her own and couldn't have given a shit to be there with me. Whereas Rosie is loving me throwing her in and riding on my back and jumping in and me catching her. It feels really nice, but I'm well aware this feeling won't last forever.

And sure enough, it all comes back to reality when Rosie says to Kit on Sunday, "You're a fake Mum."

The rational part of me knows it's button pushing but it's honestly like being shot through the heart twice. Poor Kit is pretty cut up about it. Rosie has no idea how powerful her words can be.

Chapter 22

The Children's Hearing Decision

It was the children's hearing yesterday. My mobile rings. It's the lawyer. at quarter to five.

"Sorry Nell, it was a really long hearing."

My heart sinks . Is he about to tell me the worst news of my life? Could the whole adoption order be over turned and they go back? He continues, "Really quite positive news."

Phew. I let out the biggest breath.

"The panel made a unanimous decision that direct contact should be terminated and it should be letterbox contact as originally recommended." I feel a massive weight lifting off my shoulders. I have to keep myself together as the solicitor then goes on to talk about all the legalities of the court proceedings. The system is so confusing. So even though the children's panel have made their decision our case still has to go through the court for the adoption order to be granted. The solicitor assures me it should all be straight forward as Michelle had agreed to the adoption plans. He eventually gets off the phone and I walk into the en suite in my bedroom and I just sit on the floor and cry. Once I open the flood gates, I can't get them closed. The realisation of how hard I have found the last few months really hits me. All the backwards and forwards, the unknown, the unsettled behaviours. I really hope that we can now turn a corner and Rosie can eventually be allowed to just settle into her new life without the worry of contact or fear of being taken away from her new home. I get myself together. It's amazing how many moments I've taken in the bathroom to have a cry and no one in the house would ever know. I go back downstairs where Rosie is nervously waiting to hear the outcome. I give Kit the nod to let her know all is good. The moment we decide to tell them is absolutely brilliant..

Annie is in a big bubble bath and we call a family meeting in the bathroom and Kit says , "You guys are going to be staying here. We are your forever family." Rosie is so excited.

She started screaming, "Yeah, yeah, this is the best day ever."

Kit then says , "You don't have to see your mum every month now, it will just be letters once a year until you are older or it's the right time for you."

"Yes, I know, that's what I want!" Rosie screamed. She was screaming and then jumps up and wraps her legs round me. Annie doesn't really have a clue what is going on but is joining in anyway. Kit lifts her wee naked body out the bath and we do a family hug, even the dog comes into the tiny bathroom and jumps up in celebration. It will be a moment I will never forget. Every part of me wants these girls, to take care of them, to love them, parent them, to give them their childhood, they so deserve it.

I have definitely feel lighter and happier over the last few days. I have noticed a difference with Rosie too. This morning we are walking round to school, hand in hand as we always do. We are singing, "Oh I wish it could be Christmas every day…" A woman was walking past and Rosie stopped singing but I just kept going. She looked up at me with those big brown eyes in disbelief that I would still be singing then with a big bright smile she then starts joining in again. We get to the corner of the street where we always stop, because she likes to walk the very last little bit herself. "Bye darling, have a lovely day."

"Bye," as she skips away.

Then she stops and says, "Oh wait, I forgot something." She comes running back and gives me a big hug. Honestly the love I feel t for her in that moment is like nothing I've ever experienced. I feel so blessed to have found this remarkable eight-year-old who has so much love to give. How did we get so lucky to find her? It really sets me up for the day. I feel really happy and upbeat for the rest of the day. What a contrast to a few months ago where she was telling me she hated me and I was disgusting when I walked her to school.

Chapter 23

The End of the Year

It's now the new year. I wish I was saying , *New Year New me* but its New Year, same me (just a tad bit bigger, having ate like a horse for the last few weeks). December has been a really good month for us. The girls are really settled and really enjoy being part of all the festivities. Being able to use the line, 'Santa is watching' has been brilliant. I did make the mistake of telling Annie that every time we say Santa's name that he can hear us.

Every time she see's something that she likes she says , "Santa can I have this please?" Her nursery has had lots of Christmas themed days which she just loves. Rosie's dance school wasn't able to have a show due to the Covid restrictions but parents were invited to come and see kids doing some of their classes. We go along to see her in her cheerleading class and her musical theatre class. Walking into the cheerleading class and seeing her little face watching us take our seat is just brilliant. She is proud as punch. She can't stop smiling. She concentrates so hard and performs her wee heart out, every so often she looks over to make sure we are watching her and tries to hide her grin. She is just in her element having her family here watching. Annie does the cutest thing we were arrive. . A little girl gets spooked by the audience and is crying and says she doesn't want to dance in front of people. She comes over and sits on the seat beside us. Unprompted Annie goes over and offers her a little bag of sweets. The little girl accepts and Annie just smiles and climbs back up onto my knee. It is just so lovely to watch. It is a really heart-warming moment.

The Christmas holidays are really great, although tough, given the schools and nurseries stop on the 17th of Dec so keeping the kids grounded and entertained for a whole week before Christmas is utterly exhausting. Luckily, I planned ice skating, the panto and sleep over with their cousins which all help to keep them busy and me from going insane.

At the beginning of December, we are contacted by the curator from the sheriff court who reports he needs to meet with us and the girls for the adoption petition in court. Apparently, nothing to worry about and just part of the process. Try explaining this to an eight-year-old who is living in constant fear of her new life getting ripped away from her. After I tell her he's coming to speak to us Rosie is just 100 miles an hour, completely unable to relax. She is so worried he is coming to take her away. Of course, it didn't help when he phoned twenty minutes before he was due out to see us to say he couldn't make it because he was stuck in court so she then had to wait another two days to wait to meet him. Of course, those two days were absolutely exhausting. When he then came on the Wednesday after school it really didn't help that he was dressed in a full three-piece suit and was carrying a briefcase and couldn't have looked any more official if he tried. He then decided he just wanted to speak with Kit and I and not the girls whilst at the house. This was different from what he had told me on the phone so you can imagine Rosie's anxiety at the sudden idea of him just wanting to talk only to the adults. He then asked to see Rosie in school the following week. Another week of Rosie being on high alert and not being able to relax, *Oh great,* I thought. We just had to do what we always do it this process and ride the storm for the week.

He went to see her at school and we didn't t get feedback or find out what he asked and what she said. Rosie never did tell us and we didn't want to pry. Thankfully after he saw her, she eventually settled again, just in time for the Christmas parties and fun festival things we had planned. I really thought at the time *Surely that's the last time she needs to speak to someone she doesn't know.* Turns out I was wrong. There's then a safe guarder appointed and has to speak with her before the suspension hearing that's taking place in January 2022. The suspension hearing was called as Michelle requested another hearing as she hadn't agreed with the social work recommendation of letterbox contact. I'm honestly so confused about all these different processes and who these different people are and what part of this process they come from. I get the call from the Safeguarder the day before the girls are due back to school and nursery after the New Year.

He says , "I have been appointed to ensure the girls interests are being met."

I think to myself, *Surely this has already been assessed as their interests are being met by putting them up for adoption?* As soon as I come off the phone there is a marked difference in Rosie's behaviour. She can tell straight away when it's someone official on the phone. I tell her about him straight away. He is coming to the house on Saturday. It feels strange that it is happening on a Saturday but it was already Wednesday and he had to meet with Rosie before the suspension hearing taking place on the Monday. She was now even more constant than normal, talking excessively and completely hyperactive. It is so frustrating, given how relaxed she has been over the Christmas holidays. I really wanted her to go back to school feeling refreshed. That night I put her to bed and try to reassure her she has nothing to worry about. About an hour later I think I can hear whispering coming from Rosie's room. I pop my head in her door to see what she is doing. I actually thought she was whispering to try and wake her sister up in the next room. But what I found was much worse. I can't see her so I go over to her bed and lift the covers. She is in the foetal position, under her covers just sobbing into her knees. I pull her close and she jumps up and cuddles into me and holds on for dear life. She then just lets out an almighty sob and she sobs so hard that she is struggling to breath. I've never seen her like this since she came to us. All I can do is hold her tight and try and soothe her so she can regulate her breathing again.

I say , "Are you okay?"

She replies "I feel really sad and worried but I don't know why."

I reply , "Sometimes we just need a good cry and a good cuddle." I know it is all related to the safe guarder visiting. I feel so mad. Why is the system doing this to her? Surely, they need to do more to prevent the child being this stressed? The next few nights follow the same thread, waking up with nightmares about the man taking her way, hearing her playing around in her room between two a.m. and four a.m. obviously unable to sleep. The next few days just become about getting through it and getting the visit over and done with.

Thankfully this guy hasn't come in a three-piece suit and he has brought them a magazine each and some stickers.

He is in our house for two and a half hours and Rosie really didn't say much apart from, "I hate my mum. She's disgusting. I never want to see her again."

It makes me really sad that she feels that's what she has to say. I don't believe she does feel that way about Michelle but she obviously feels she has to say it so she doesn't get taken away. It's just so sad they have put her in this position where she feels she needs to say this. This whole process has just been so unfair on her. Anyway, thankfully it's done. All the court stuff starts in the next few weeks. Thankfully, the girls know nothing about this and can just get on with life as normal.

I'm going to meet my boss tomorrow to talk about my return-to-work plan. I can't believe it's been six months since we have had the girls. I feel so much has happened in such a short space of time. I'm looking forward to having another purpose instead of just being the person that cleans, cooks, does the food shop, speaks to the social workers, repeat. I plan to go back three days a week to begin with and I can still do the drop off and pick up from school. The girls will be none the wiser which will be good. So many times, people spoke about losing a bit of yourself that you will never get back, grieving your old life and the old you. I naively thought, *My life won't be that different. I will be the same me.* What a complete fool I was. Don't get me wrong, I love the girls and don't regret adopting these two beautiful little humans and bringing them into our lives. But oh my God, I didn't appreciate the time I had before my life changed. To eat whenever I wanted, to go exercise, to work late, to meet for a coffee, to go for a night out, to just go to the cinema or out for dinner whenever we wanted was luxury. I find myself jealous of kid-less friends and neighbours and sometimes just find myself wishing I could just have that back for one day. The enormous, constant responsibility of children was not something I can say I fully considered or understood. I also find it so tough being far away from my mum and my best friend. When we pulled out of my mum's drive to come back to Edinburgh after spending a few days there over Christmas, I had this overwhelming feeling of sadness and homesick. The practical and emotional help from them is something I just don't have in Edinburgh. Even on that day I didn't get a chance to just be upset or sad about missing home because the girls just don't leave me alone. The only way to get alone time to be with my own thoughts and to have little secret cries was to do the biggest Christmas clean-up of the house. Doing housework is the only time they leave me alone. I suppose it was quite cleansing to get a clean house. So different from before where I would lie on the couch, binge-watch Netflix and just cry and eat junk food all day until I got over it.

Chapter 24

The Lovely Bits That Make You Forget the Hard Bits

This morning was just so heart-warming. It's little moments like this morning that start to really make me feel like the attachment is getting so much stronger with Annie. We are walking into the nursery, hand in hand as we do most mornings when we park up on the street outside. She has her hair in pigtails and her big cosy winter jacket on looking so cute. We get to the gate, and there are a few other kids and their parents dropping them. Due to Covid rules parents aren't allowed inside the building. So, we have to meet the nursery teacher at the outside gate and pass over the kids at that point.

Annie runs in the gate to get to Miss Williams and I shout, "Have fun." The gate gets closed and the Miss Williams starts turning to walk the group of kids into the building. Annie turns and notices the gate has been shut and she shouts, "Mummy Nell , Mummy Nell. Please open the gate so I can give her a cuddle." She looks like she is going to burst into tears.

Another little boy who is watching her then starts copying her. "Let me cuddle my mummy," he also shouts. They all start running back towards the gate. Miss Williams turns and laughs at the chaos around her. She opens the gate and Annie comes running up and I scoop her into my arms.

"Have a great day baby girl. Remember I love you," I whisper into her ear.

She replies, "Member I love you."

We both rub our noses together and say, "Noses," in harmony and then I put her down and she happily runs back in the gate doing a silly little dance/run. I exchange a few pleasantries with the other parents 'oh what are they like, so cute' kind of comments and then I just stand and watch as they all run into nursery together, all giggling and smiling. The love I feel for this tiny human is insane. I have to try and contain myself until I got to my car, I am really filling up. On my drive back to the house I have a little cry. It is happy tears and feeling of relief, gratitude and love. Little moments like these make all the tough bits worthwhile.

Today is the suspension hearing regarding the last decisions made in the hearing, which was to terminate face-to-face contact with Michelle.. The kids are none the wiser these hearings are taking place and Kit and I don't have to attend as our solicitor attends on our behalf, thankfully. I don't think Rosie would be able to function at all if she knew what was going on in the background. The decision of the last panel was upheld and there was no change. The safe guarder calls me before the hearing, just as I arrive home after the nursery drop-off to update me of his meetings with the social worker and Michelle. The phone call lasts well over an hour. He speaks at great length of his phone calls and meeting with Michelle. He relays that Michelle really just wants to know the girls are well and happy.

He says , "I've seen a lot of children in a lot of different situations over the years and honestly, they are both so happy and so loved. They couldn't be any happier." He said that's really all she was concerned about. In that moment I feel really sorry for Michelle. She has lost the two most precious things in her life. The safe guarder is very sympathetic to her circumstances. I am really quite pulled into his way of thinking. And then I remind myself that I now parent the eight-year-old who has been so negatively impacted by her behaviours and poor choices. I am sympathetic of Michelle's situation, I always have been, right from the start of the process but Rosie and Annie are my priority and their needs need to come first. I can only imagine how difficult it is for Michelle. . I have no doubt once Rosie firmly believes she will live here forever and Michelle doesn't have control over taking her away from her new life that she will eventually decide she wants contact or some more questions answered but until that point comes Rosie needs to know we have her back and it will be her call about contact. No one else's. My hope for the future is that one day Rosie is secure in the fact this is her home and she could speak with Michelle and Michelle is in a place when she can be consistent and healthy and it can be positive for Rosie. Time will tell.

Chapter 25

Thank God for *Matilda* and Davina

Annie's new favourite thing to do is watch films. Over Christmas she became obsessed with *E.T* and *Ghostbusters* and now it's *Matilda.* I collect her from nursery and the first thing she said was, "Can we go home and watch *Tilda?*" As soon as she gets home, I put it on the TV for her. She had watched the first half the last night so she gets her blanket and gets cosy on the sofa and starts watching the second half. I could sit and watch her watching the TV all night. She is so emersed in the film. She stops for dinner and then asks to watch it for a second time. She doesn't get bored once watching it the second time. I can't get Rosie to watch it at all. She tends to shy away from any movies that have mean people, or if it's to do with families. She prefers sci-fi type movies that couldn't be at all relatable.

Thankfully Annie is going through this movie stage 'cause I've done something to my back and it's in bloody agony. I can barely move. My mental health gets seriously impacted if my physical health is off coulter. I'm like a bear with a sore head. I booked an emergency appointment with a chiropractor. I would have paid £500 in that moment for the pain to be removed. He explained what I had done to one of the muscles round my spine and that's what was causing the pain and discomfort. The good news was once he manipulated me it did give me instant relief but after a few hours it soon crept back up. I feel every little ache in my body right now, like I'm so aware of everything. I do wonder/worry if my body is responding physically to the stress I have been under in this six-month period? The last week has been tough enough with a sore back, I can't imagine being in my new role as a mum with debilitating physical health problems. It would turn me into a monster.

I take the girls to my mum's for the weekend. It is such a good weekend. I feel so exhausted with my back and haven't been sleeping well. I honestly feel lighter as soon as I arrive at my mum's. She's so good at not just knowing when I need help but how to help.

"Just sit down and I will do it," she says as I go to get up to do one of the many things the kids ask me to do. "Go out for a walk with Davina in the morning and I will watch the kids," she says. It's like music to my ears. Davina has been my best friend since I was fourteen. She lives just around the corner from my mum. I'm so delighted at the prospect of 1. Having a lie-in as my mum gets up and sees to the kids and 2. Having a walk with my pal with no kids in the morning.

I'm so happy to meet Davina at the end of the street and see her big smile. She's going through a hard time just now with trying to get pregnant. She really desperately wants to start a family. I try to tell her in the most supportive way that now that I have kids I look back on the free time I used to have and wonder why I didn't take more advantage of it. I know it must be hard to think like that, especially when all you want is a family. I wish I had really listened and understood when people tried to explain it to me. Never did I imagine I would be so excited to go for an hour's walk with Davina around the park. I love meeting with Davina. There's something so special about having a friend that's known you through all your different phases in life. She knew me when I was super annoying teenager, when I was 'straight' and when I was child-free. There's a deeper understanding and appreciation for each other. I'm just free to be me, every little part. I don't need to put a face on and agree with how much joy children bring. I can be really honest about the exhaustion, the hard bits, the rejection along with the joys, the amazing bits, the lovely bits. No matter what I say, she never judges me and always sees the best of me. I feel very blessed. I must have done something really wonderful in a previous life to have landed Davina as a best pal.

I feel refreshed after my walk with Davina. My afternoon is then spent with my other two best pals from school(also live beside my mum) with their kids. The difference in the morning to the afternoon is like night and day. I don't really get the chance to properly catch up with Cat and Lizzy because all of our attention is 100% taken up by the kids. I might not feel as refreshed by my afternoon walk but I definitely feel better. Seeing Cat and Lizzy having the same struggles, the same cheek, the same defiance that I have with the girls makes me feel dare I say it, 'normal'. I get so caught up in the whole 'adoption' process that you start to feel different from the rest but actually being there and seeing how every other mother interacts with their children and hearing them share the common moans, "I'm exhausted, they are getting on my last nerve. Why did we have kids?" Etcetera. It's refreshing, just in a different way from my walk with Davina.

That same evening, we stay at my mum's for dinner and I decide to make the drive home later so I can just put the kids straight to bed and Rosie won't miss her swimming lesson in the morning. My mum invited Gary and Kim, my brother and sister-in-law for dinner. Gary and I used to be really close, but over the last year there has been a real distance between us, Covid probably played a big factor in that. At first, I felt really hurt and sad by it but I then realised I stopped trying too. I really missed him, at first, but more recently I have to be honest, I actually haven't had the head space to be thinking about it, not with everything going on with our expanding family and all the legal complications, it hasn't left me with much head space for anything else. But tonight, seeing Gary and Kim and being with them made me think differently. Tonight, when they arrived at my mum's it was awkward chit-chat at first. It never used to be awkward at all. I can't even remember how we got to this point. Kim tries, but I can tell it's a strain for her too. I know she wants thinks to be better between Gary and I. I think to myself, *Why has it got to this point? Things used to be so easy?* It makes me feel sad. I feel sorry for my mum. She's obviously invited them because she wants things to be better for all of us. I try really hard and eventually Gary warms up to speaking to me and I feel the tension ease off. I get a glimmer of how it used to be and it reminds me of how much I miss the connection we once had. I think to myself how lucky I am to have the option right in front of me to have a relationship with my brother. Rosie and Annie have had that option removed. They won't grow up with their brother and have the opportunity. I count my blessings in that moment of thought. I know my brother feels like I drifted and I need to take responsibility for my part, as well as my stubborn brother needs to take responsibility for his part.

I make a pledge, "Get back on track, be a sister, you've only got one brother." I drive home feeling happier that we spent time together. I sent a text to Gary *It was good to see you guys tonight. I miss it.* That's my olive branch… He replies. I'm delighted. I realise how much I missed them and love them

Chapter 26

This Sore Back

My back isn't any better. I have completely and utterly done it in! I'm like a bear with a sore head. My poor children and wife! It's nearly been a week now. Kit has had to dress Annie in the morning and do more of the practical hands-on stuff because I just haven't been able to. My mood has been so low. I hate feeling this way. I have been so short and snappy with the kids and Kit. Yesterday and this morning when I have taken Annie to nursery, she has been really teary, came running back to me and needed lots of reassurance going in. Miss Williams asked if there's anything different about her routines or anything.

I said, "No there's nothing particularly different. The only thing I can think of is I have a sore back so I haven't been doing lots of the practical things I would normally do like get her dressed, bath her, and I haven't been able to lift her as much."

Miss Williams said, "Sometimes it can just be the simplest things that throw them off but it might well be that change has unsettled her." I instantly feel awful. I know that as well as not being readily available to do the practical things that I have also emotionally not been as readily available because I have been so grumpy because of my back. There's that guilt creeping in again. This tiny little human now relies on me. She has trusted me to look after her, she has slowly but surely allowed me to bring down her walls and let me care for her. How could I be so wrapped up in myself to let it impact her? I need to do better. I lift her up in my arms and hold her tight to my body.

"Aw my girl, let's cuddle." My back is screaming in pain but I don't dare let it win.

Through her tears she said, "I just needed to give you a cuddle Mummy Nell." My back is screaming, 'Put down this weight' but my heart is screaming, 'You won't get this time back ever again, ignore the pain'. After her cuddle she is ready to go with Miss Williams quite happily. On the car journey back home to take Rosie to school I reflect on how I have been over the last few days. The guilt eats me up. I have been so short with Rosie too. They do not deserve this, Nell. I need to be less moody. It's not their fault I've done my back in. We walk round to school hand in hand and I'm so aware of the throbbing back pain but I really put a face on, smile, chat and try to be more playful. She responds so well. I make a pledge to continue with my new attitude when I pick them up. The evening goes so much better. They are both much more relaxed because I am much cheerier and more relaxed. The realisation of how much they rely on me to be consistent in my mood and presentation is so important to their mood and presentation. Gone are the days of moping around feeling sorry for yourself when you have an injury. Now I'm a mum I need to suck it up and keep going. And actually, once the kids are in bed, my mood has actually improved by pretending to be on my A game. Positive thoughts, positive mindset, positive behaviour change. Looks like those psychologists have been right all along.

Chapter 27

Rosie Turns Nine

It's Rosie's ninth birthday.. She has been talking about her birthday since the day I met her. We have been so worried about what to do to celebrate, her expectations are so high. Because of Covid restrictions we can only have a few people over to the house.

She said to me the other night, "I wish I was at my old school again. I had friends there."

I said, "It's hard starting a new school and making new friends darling."

She replied, "No one plays with me. The girls have a group and don't let anyone in. If I had still been at my own school they would have wanted to come to my party and buy me a present." My heartaches for her. I so desperately want her to make friends. She so desperately wants to have a friend.

She says, "I don't think anyone will buy me a present."

I reply and say, "Don't worry you have only been at your new school for five months, you are still settling in and getting to know people. You have your cousins and your friend Sylvia (little girl who is our neighbour) and family coming who all love you and can't wait to give you gifts." I wish so badly I could make school life easier for her.

I pick her up from school in the afternoon.. I'm standing at the school gate with the Angus. Angus loves coming to school pick up. The lollipop man always has dog treats for him. . I'm hoping with every part of me that the kids have been nice and at least wished her a happy birthday. She comes running out the playground with a gift bag and the biggest smile on her face.

"Mummy look my friend Ashely got me all of these amazing presents." My heart is so happy, I could cry happy tears to see her this happy. She shouts, "Ashley come and see my mummy."

I said, "Oh wow, that's amazing. So, kind." The street is really busy and lots of kids and parents walking out and crossing over and going in all directions. Ashley crosses the busy road at the lollipop man and is on the other side.

Rosie is shouting, "Bye Ashley." Ashley is waving bye.

I impulsively say to Rosie, "Would Ashley like to come to your party tomorrow?"

Rosie replies so quickly, "Yes yes yes Mummy. Ashley," she shouts across the busy road. "Do you want to come to my party tomorrow?"

"When is it?" Ashely shouts over the traffic.

"Tomorrow twelve o'clock at 126 Smallville Road. I live across the road from the park."

Ashley a bit confused shouts, "Okay I will need to ask my mum." She starts running home. I'm frantically thinking, *Oh no, she's never going to come.*

I say to Rosie, "Shall we cross over and run after her and go with her to ask her mum if she can come?"

"Yes." We frantically wait for a space and run across the road.

I say, "Run ahead and shout at her." I'm very aware of other children and parents looking at us wondering what on earth is going on. Angus is dragging me along by the lead and Rosie is sprinting ahead shouting after her. She eventually gets Ashley's attention and Ashley stops.

I catch up and say, "We thought it might be a good idea if we walk you to your door and I could exchange numbers with your mum and see if you can come over to the party tomorrow?." Ashley looks at me like I'm a crazy lady and she would be right. I am a crazy lady desperate for Rosie to have a friend. We walk Ashley right to her door. Ashley's mum looks at us the exact same way Ashley did.

I say, "Hello, sorry to bombard you at your door. Rosie was just so delighted with her present from Ashley, she would love it if Ashley could come over for her little party in the house tomorrow. It's just a small thing."

Ashley's mum's face softens, "Oh that sounds lovely. When is it?"

Rosie replies immediately, "It's from twelve till two."

"Ahh," Ashley's mum says. "You normally have gymnastics then but would you prefer the party?" Ashley softly nods her head. I'm very aware of the pressure we are probably putting on them and Ashley is probably thinking, *This mental woman I don't know has chased me home from school.*

I say, "Why don't we exchange numbers and I can text you all the details and if she can make it then we would love to have her."

Ashley's Mum smiles. "Ahh that's perfect." We exchange numbers and Rosie and I get going. We walk home hand in hand. She says, "That was so lucky we caught her; I really hope she comes." I think to myself, *You have no idea how much I want her to come.*

Much to Rosie's delight, Ashley's mum texts me back to say that Ashley would love to come. Rosie is beyond excited! I am just so happy for her. Her wee party is just perfect. She's in her element showing her room off and playing the scavenger hunt games. Everything Ashley does Rosie wants to copy. It's so sweet to watch her. She is honestly so well behaved the whole weekend and she keeps saying, "I'm just so grateful for this party. I think this might be my best birthday ever." She just fills my heart with joy. It makes me want to give her everything in my power. My love for her grows and grows every day with every new experience.

As expected now the spotlight has been on Rosie for her birthday. Annie has been so jealous and constantly naughty over the last week. I said to my mum when I phoned her the other night that I felt like Annie was ADHD on speed. She has just been a nightmare to manage. Back to saying no to everything, doing the opposite of what she has been told and having to be physically lifted to get her from A to B, e.g., refusing to come into the house, refusing to get in the car, refusing to leave other people's houses, running around the swimming pool changing rooms butt naked trying to hide from me as I try to catch her while trying to keep my own dignity and not let my towel fall down. Why do these incidents need to happen when the changing rooms are crammed with folk. As much as I enjoyed seeing Rosie so happy and enjoy her birthday, I'm so looking forward to getting back to normality and for Annie's jealousy to subside. She is one feisty little girl. Right now, it can be so cute but I often think about what teenage Annie will be like. Boy are we in for a bumpy ride.

Chapter 28

Sometimes You Just Have to Remove the Middle Man

I get a voicemail from our lawyer..

"Hi Nell, Chris here. There's been a bit of a development in the case that I need to discuss with you that's come to light at the sheriff court this morning."

My first thought, *What the hell has happened? A development? If it was a good development surely, he would have said on the voicemail.* My brain was working at 90mph. Of course, trying to call back is a nightmare. He's possibly the busiest person I know. The voicemail was at ten a.m. and I eventually get to speak to him at three-thirty p.m. You can imagine the number of scenarios that ran through my head as possibilities in that time frame. To be fair to Chris he did try and call back at lunchtime but I had just bought a car from the chattiest Glaswegian in the world and he happened to call me at the same time the lawyer had tried to call me back. I did attempt three times to get Tony off the phone but he wasn't getting the hint.

"Hi Nell, sorry I'm just out another hearing and this is the first chance I've had to call you back."

I say, "Aw no worries, Chris." Acting like I haven't been insanely running through all the worst possibilities in my head all day. I wish I was that relaxed person that I was portraying, but my crazy irrational brain always takes over.

Chris goes on to say, "We started the court case today at the sheriff court as you know. Michelle's lawyer shared that Michelle is not going to contest the adoption order." It was a weird feeling listening to Chris continue to talk about the process and what it all means. All I could think about is Michelle and how hard it must be for her. I obviously was delighted that things would hopefully be made permanent sooner rather than later but I felt mixed. The following day, the girls' new social worker, Linda called me to get an update on how the girls are. She asked how they are connecting with the rest of the family. I went on to tell her how much they love being part of a wider larger family with Nana, Granny and all their aunties, uncles and cousins. Linda told me that Michelle was very isolated and the kids would not have experienced lots of family before. I instantly felt guilty for all the moaning I do and realised just how lucky we are to have loving, supportive family and friends around us and the kids. Again, it left me wondering how Michelle was coping with her little baby. She must be feeling so isolated and alone and probably has done for her whole life. That's why she has probably made such poor choices in partners. It was a surreal moment for me. I felt really lucky and grateful for the support I have around me. It made me think of my own mum with two kids under two and at the age of twenty years old, on her own, hardly any money and ultimately not a lot of hope. I have no idea how she got through it. I think she should write a book. I would definitely read it.

I really hope that one day in the future when Rosie is ready that she will reconnect with Michelle and it be as positive as it can be. It would be so good for both of them.

Unfortunately, a few days later Chris called me again, things didn't remain as simple as the original phone call.

Chris said, "Michelle isn't contesting the adoption order but she is fighting for sibling contact to be put in the order as a condition, this would mean we would have to go through the full court case." As the story unfolds Chris explains that he feels like Michelle is in a direct fight with social work which appears to be impacting on her continued disagreement with the adoption order and this is why this new issue is now coming up. Everything felt like it was going up in the air again. Rosie was sensing things were going on by the amount of phone calls I was getting and going away to privately chat. I feel angry at social work. I agree with Chris, I also think Michelle is fighting the recommendations because it is social works recommendations and she has been impacted by social work recommendations her whole life. I know Michelle loves Rosie and Annie; I know there's no way she would be wanting her kids to be feeling this unsettled or for them to go through any more heartbreak. I decide to take matters into my own hands. I'm tired of listening to social workers. I decide to write directly to Michelle and get Chris to send our letter directly to Michelle's solicitor so it's nothing to do with social work.

This is our letter to Michelle:

Dear Michelle ,

It's Nell and Kit here. We wanted to write to you so you have a direct message from us without social work being the middle man and what we say doesn't get misunderstood. We first want to thank you for bringing such amazing little humans into this world. They really are little rays of sunshine and we feel blessed to have them as part of our lives. I know this process hasn't been easy for you or the girls. I can only imagine how difficult it must be for you to hear that Rosie isn't in a place where she wants to see you. But we want you to know that we firmly believe once Rosie truly settles and believes this is her forever home and she won't have to move again she will want to reconnect with you. It just has to be at a time that feels right for her.

When there haven't been stressful conversations about contact with social workers or safe guarders and it's just in her day-to day life, she does talk positively about you. She will often say, "I got my hair from my mum."

Which we always reply with, "You have beautiful, thick hair just like your mum. You are both so lucky to have such gorgeous hair." This always makes her smile. She will often tell us a story about when she was really little and you were filming her and she was asking for pizza for her breakfast. Retelling this story is a really happy memory for her and she talks about how funny it was because she kept saying it and you were laughing. We feel it's important for you to know that we are absolutely keeping you alive in her story as much as we understand there were really tough times for both of you, we know there were really special times too.

We know that you have been worried that due to the children's hearing decision to terminate contact and there not being a condition of contact on the order at the moment that that might mean it has closed the door completely. We want to assure you that when the girls are ready and want to reconnect that we will fully support the girls to do so. The social work system and the legal system has been difficult for us all to navigate through. It has been particularly tough on Rosie. Having social workers, safe guarders and curators from the court coming back and forward to meet her at the house and school has really had such a negative impact on her and we believe we are both on the same page about not wanting to put her through any more turmoil with the system and want her to settle, grow and flourish into being even more amazing than she already is.

We know it is important for you to promote Rosie and Annie's relationship with Josh and we completely understand it. Right now, Rosie has just too many unresolved feelings about Josh's birth and the idea of Josh living with you is hard for her. We believe in time when

Rosie is settled and is able to accept seeing photo updates of Josh, she will be more open to the idea of contact with him. When I showed her the photos of Josh when he was a few weeks old it was really distressing for her. Our fear is if contact is forced on her by the system that she will pull back further and we certainly don't want that for her or you and Josh.

This is a letter from our hearts to yours (adoptive mums to birth mum). We love Rosie and Annie and will always, always protect them, care for them and try our hardest to offer them every opportunity life throws at them. We want you to know we promote a positive and open story about their journey so far in life and the place you will always have as their birth mum. We just want you to know that even though she doesn't want contact now doesn't mean it's closed. It just means we are trying our hardest to listen to her, hear her and support her with what she needs just now. And when she comes to the point of wanting contact, please be assured we will listen, we will hear her and we will take action to ensure it happens.

Kindest wishes

Nell and Kit

Within a few days on sending our letter we got a reply from Michelle:

Dear Nell and Kit, I appreciate you taking the time out your day to write to me personally, I would first like to say how much I appreciate all you do for my girls and thank you for the lovely photos of them and updates it's very much appreciated, I was very pleased to hear at the last meeting how thriving they are and how settled they've became at your family home. Breaks my heart to know they're not coming home with me as you can imagine but it does bring me great comfort to know I never have to go to my bed worried about who they're with, and know you'll both take good care of them, I'll always be grateful for everything use have done and are doing for my girls. I made a lot of mistakes but there's not a day that doesn't go by where I do not miss them and wish I had the head then that I do now for them beautiful girls. I would like you to make Rosie and Annie aware, when u feel the time is right, that I was promised by social work I would be the one to tell them about Josh and loads of authorities are aware that this is the case, I made them aware of how unsettled it would make Rosie and felt it was right to come from me, they went ahead and did it without me anyways, I never wanted them to find out like that. I have tried my best to take them home, I never want them to feel like I never loved them, and I don't want them to feel like I only love Josh because that is not the case. I fully believe you both do have my children's best interests at heart and if they ever wanted to see me or Josh, I do now believe you would promote that. I believe you will promote the sibling relationship with Josh. I would never force my children to see me or Josh, Rosie has every right to feel the way she does, but I just wanted to do all I can now for them, as you can understand, and never want them to wake up one day and think I want to see my mum and Josh but I can't. I have only ever wanted to leave the door open for them to do so. I miss them very much and I hope they're doing okay.

Michelle

I was sat on the couch when I opened Michelle's letter and I just sobbed. I cried for her, I cried for the girls and I cried for us. I know she's made some terrible mistakes and wasn't able to give the girls the care they needed but I can feel the love she has for them in her reply and to live with that guilt must be so hard.

It's a few days later, and I speak to Chris on the phone. He says, "In all the years I've worked in this area I have never had any parent write directly to birth parents during this process. I will be honest Nell, , when you first told me you were doing it, I was very sceptical but you have definitely proved me wrong."

I said, "I wasn't even sure myself Chris if it would have any impact but I was just sick of being on the outside looking in and feeling like our voice was missing from the process."

He replies, "Your voice was most definitely heard Nell. I will be in touch in next week once it goes back to court and it should be pretty straight forward if there is nothing being contested in the adoption order."

I say, "Fingers crossed," and we end the call. Even though it seems like it should all go smoothly I have learned from this process to never take anything for granted as so many changes have happened along the way. I don't feel like we are quite out of the woods yet.

Chapter 29

Thank You For Being my Mummy

I am putting on Annie's boots for her trying to get us out the door on time for nursery and out of the blue she says, "Thank you for being my mummy."

I stop in my tacks. I don't think I will ever forget this moment. We are in the hallway; she is sitting on the wooden storage box with her little red *Minnie Mouse* jacket as I'm putting on her little brown boots. I feel overwhelmed with love for this tiny little human, so cute and innocent.

I reply, "You're welcome. I love being your mummy."

To which she says, "Will you be my mummy until I die?." The finality of her statement made me laugh.

I say, "Yes, forever."

And she says, "And then when I die you will be sad but it will be okay." The brain of a four-year-old is so funny. She must have heard something about dying recently, she's made a few statements like this. .

I say, "You aren't going to die any time soon. You will live a very long happy life." She looks at me smiles and finishes off our conversation with, "Yes 'cause I'm only the number four."

There seems to be a lot of processing happening for Annie in the last few weeks and her understanding of living with us forever and us being her mummies appears to be taking shape in her little mind. It feels pretty incredible to be reaching this point with her. When I think back to the beginning it was so tough watching how confused she was about her life and where she belonged. I'm so pleased all her jigsaw pieces are starting to fit together nicely in her little head.

We have also started this funny thing of sometimes saying grace at the dinner table. We are in no way religious or anything like that, I just thought it would be funny one night when we had the kids at my mum's for dinner. The kids now love it and keep saying let's do grace when we all sit at the dinner table.

Tonight, as we are all sat at the table all nearly finished Rosie said, "Oh we forgot to say grace."

Kit said, "Okay do it now then."

Both Rosie and Annie then started talking over each other trying to do it.

I said, "One at a time."

Annie then said, "Grace is having this family and Angus." And she hung onto my arm and pulled herself closer to me. It was so cute.

Rosie then said, "I'm so thankful to be adopted into this amazing family." I feel such a sense of pride and wholeness in that moment.

I then said, "I'm so grateful to have such special children in my life. I'm so proud of you. You are both little rays of sunshine." Seeing their faces light up in these moments is comparable to nothing else.

It is really tough being a parent, especially being an adoptive parent but it is just so worth it. It's these moments that make the hard moments worth it, like when Rosie decided it would be okay to take a knife and carve a massive X and a love heart into my mum's kitchen worktop because she was 'bored' or when Annie decides she wants to burst into our bedroom at three a.m. put the light on and shout, "Wake up you sleepy head."

Chapter 30

Adoption Order is Granted

Chris phones. "Today it has been confirmed that the adoption order has been granted in court and it's all official now. Congratulations". I struggle to take it in. I feel weird. Family and friends are texting me with similar messages "Amazing news, what are you doing to celebrate?."

It's a strange feeling. I feel relieved it's now all official and we don't need to deal with social workers and the legal system but it's really bittersweet. I feel it's not quite right to be celebrating straight away. What is meant to be a joyous day for us is probably the worst day of Michelle's life. The kids officially staying with us forever means this is the day she officially won't have her kids returned to her care. I can't imagine what she's going through.

For the moment the girls will have twice yearly letterbox contact where they will exchange letters and photos with Michelle. I hope with all my heart Michelle is able to keep on a good path and they will establish contact and it be a positive experience for all of them in the future when Rosie is ready of course.

To celebrate we have decided that tomorrow we will mark the girl's height on the fence and we will do it every six months. Marking another milestone in this journey so far. It's incredible to think it's only been seven months. I wonder what the next seven months is going to be like…

As I sit here after putting them to bed, I reflect on what I have learned in the last seven months:

1. Parenting is something you *cannot* prepare for. When I think back to the first three months, I can't believe how exhausted, unorganised and ill-prepared I was and to an extent still am. I have learned that I need to be okay with feeling like I'm winging it *all the time.*
2. I can go from feeling such pride and joy in something they do to very quickly feeling exacerbated by something they do all in the space of thirty minutes.
3. The realisation of just how hard it was for my own mum and how much I respect her. Parenting is hard and I'm still astounded she did it by herself at the age of twenty with two kids under two with not two pennies to rub together.
4. No matter how many times you say wipe your bottom, flush the toilet and wash your hands after you have had a pee, she will forget (rather decide to not bother) at least two out of the three instructions and I have to intervene every time.

5. No matter how mad they make me, it doesn't last for long (well if I'm on my period it can last a good bit longer).
6. Taking time for myself is crucial. Signing up for the marathon was the best decision I made. I love going out running for escapism, even before adopting the kids. Signing up for the marathon gave me a strict training schedule to stick to, it's made me feel fitter and healthier and it has given me a sense of self which you definitely lose a bit of when you become a parent and that becomes your main focus. Plus, it's also been great listening to audio books and podcasts about adoption, trauma and parenting which has been super helpful.
7. I would make a really good doctor, especially an Australian one (I don't know why but I always use an Australian accent). I've played doctors that many times with Annie that I feel I'm prepared for any situation that arises, whether that is a sore tummy because little aliens are living in your tummy, or your bottom has fallen off and you have lost it in a bike accident or all your toes have broken off because the cat chewed them. Playing games and spending time with them can sometimes feel relentless but there has never once been a time where they haven't enjoyed it. I endeavour to keep it up.

Chapter 31

Mother's Day

I pick Rosie up from brownies.. She normally comes running out being really loud and excitable but tonight couldn't be more different. She comes out walking quietly. Her little friend Sylvia who I am picking up too comes out smiling and shows me the Mother's Day card she has made for her mum. I know straight away this will have been a tough thing for Rosie.

We drop Sylvia off and then I ask, "Are you okay?."

She replies, "Yeah fine."

I say, "It's okay to feel a bit sad about Mother's Day. You are allowed to feel weird about it and sad because you miss your birth mum."

She replies, "Okay," as her eyes start to fill up but she so desperately doesn't want to engage in the conversation.

We get back to the house and she runs in and goes straight upstairs which is very unlike her. She normally wants to tell us every little detail about brownies and use every stalling tactic in the books to delay going to bed. Kit goes up to say goodnight and is back down within a minute. "Wow that's a first that she couldn't wait to get rid of me." I tell Kit what's happened.

I leave it twenty minutes and then go up to see her. I go in quietly and find her lying in her bed crying quietly.

I say, "Can I give you a hug?" She nods. I go onto her bed and I give her a hug and a little kiss on her nose.

I say, "I'm sorry you are feeling sad darling. You know you can talk to us about anything."

She looks at me with her beautiful big eyes and whispers , "I know. I just feel sad about missing my old life. I miss everything. My old school, my friends. Sometimes it's just harder."

I give her a squeeze and say, "I can't imagine how you feel darling, it must be tough. Know that we are here."

She smiles at me as tears are rolling down her face and she turns and says , "I know. Goodnight." It breaks my heart leaving her, knowing she doesn't want comfort from me is hard to swallow. I so badly want to hug her so tight and tell her everything will be okay and that I will make it okay and make it all better. But I can't. I just need to be here and waiting for when she does want comfort. It just breaks my heart that I can't help her.

She never did say what was wrong and chose not to talk about it with me. I attempt to ask but she is very closed down. I ask her if she wants to write a letter to her birth mum or make a picture and she could send them when it's letterbox contact.

She replies , "No I don't want to." I reassure her she can talk to us about anything. She replies , "Yes I know."

It makes me realise how far away she is from us and how little we know of what is really going on in her head. She is always striving for attention and it feels like she talks all the time but when it actually comes down to the real raw stuff we are not in her circle of trust yet. We really are in a powerless position. Just watching these things roll out and not being able to do anything about it or have any positive impact is painful. I know she talks all the time but I think she talks with the constant nonsense chatter because if she stops and allows herself to think it would all just be too painful for her.

The lead up to Mother's Day isn't as bad as I had thought it would be. Luckily, I am into doing my own woodwork projects so decide to make my mum a planter for her garden. I ask the kids if they want to help. Rosie jumps at the chance. She loves using the measuring tape and drawing the lines to where I need to cut. The project turns out lovely.

She says to me, "Why are you making something and not just buying something?"

I reply , "Giving someone a homemade gift is so much better. The time and effort speaks volumes to the person receiving the gift." She fell silent and looks to be deep in thought.

She then says , "Can I make Mummy Kit a gift?."

"Of course you can," I said with a smile. "That's a lovely idea." I help her make a plague and she decides to stick wooden letters saying 'Family' and make a little washing line and we print our first family photo and she glues it to the washing line. It really is lovely. She is very proud of her work. It is lovely to see how excited she is to give her gift to Mummy Kit. It's the morning of Mother's Day, Rosie gets up really early and goes downstairs and makes a big sign that says Happy Mother's Day. I am really surprised. It is very sweet of her. I know Mother's Day must be hard for her. We all go out as a family of four for afternoon tea which is a good shout because both of them absolutely love eating cakes and they demolish the cake stand. Annie doesn't have a clue what is going on but is happy to be celebrating going for afternoon tea. Rosie says to me just before she goes to bed, "Is it hard being a mum?" Her question takes me by surprise.

I say , "Yeah it's hard, but I'm trying my best."

She replies , "You don't have to try your best; you are the best." Sometimes it's like I'm speaking to an old woman with a wise soul in a 9 year old body then I remember she has been through so much heartache already in her little life that she probably is very wise before her time. I kiss her goodnight " I love you Rosie, you are one in a million". "Night Mum".

Chapter 32

Starting to Feel Normal

My mum is here staying for a few nights as Kit is away abroad with work this week. I always look forward to my mum coming. Not only is she great with helping with the girls but she also helps with cooking, walking the dog and my most favourite thing is having her around just to have a chat and a cup of tea with. She always buys the girls lots of clothes, so Rosie is in her element when Nana arrives with all the clothes and she gets to try them all on and does a fashion show. I love that my mum does this. She has a knack for knowing what will fit and also what they will like and look good in. I'm not into shopping at all and I'm not very good at picking nice outfits the way my mum is. Rosie's little face is lit up like a Christmas light when she trying everything on and my mum is making a fuss of her." Woot woo, Beautiful" I can hear her say. Annie is still just a bit too little but she is also loving doing a little fashion parade copying her big sister and showing her new clothes off. It's great to see my mum getting to know the kids better too. The kids were just as excited as I was about her coming.

Rosie says , "Can it just be Nana that comes to pick me up from school and walk me to school?."

I say , "Yes if Nana is okay with that then it's okay with me."

My mum says , "Oh I would love to." Rosie looks delighted. After the fashion show I am tidying up around the living room and Rosie is following me around and she eventually says , "I had another Nana before my new Nana."

Her comment took me by surprise. I say , "Yes, was that your birth mum's mum?"

she says , "Yes but she couldn't handle us and would get angry with Annie"

I reply , "That must have been scary."

She replies, "No it wasn't scary, just wasn't fun." And she then skipped off to go and talk to Nana and Annie. She must be reflecting on the difference. I go to put the kettle on and chat with my mum.

She says , "Do you want to go and play football tonight and I can watch the girls?" Normally Kit and I do alternate weeks at football and one of us watches the kids.

I reply , "are you sure?."

She says , "Yes, they seem pretty settled. They will be fine and I will be fine and you aren't away that long that if it is a disaster you can be back to sort it."

I feel pretty confident they will behave for my mum and that my mum won't be shy about keeping them in check. And true to her word, the kids were absolutely fine. I came home from football; the kids were in bed asleep and my mum was chilling on her iPad in the living room. For the first time it started to feel like we were beginning to be like more like a 'normal' family where you leave the kids with grandparents and all is fine. It feels like a milestone in our journey. Of course, Annie pushed it a little bit but what kid doesn't? Even that felt normal.

It's Tuesday morning and my mum walks Rosie to school and picks her up again.

As the bell goes Rosie is running to the line and shouting at the top of her voice for the whole playground to hear, "Bye Nana love you." And then at the end of the day she comes running out shouting, "Nana." And gives her a massive hug. It looks like she is proud to show the world that she has a Nana that is picking her up.

Chapter 33

It's Okay to Be Honest

I am speaking to my best friend, Davina on the phone. She had a miscarriage last year and they have struggled to conceive since. Davina really is the nicest human on this planet. Being friends with her makes me be a better person. She is telling me that she feels like the worst person in the world. She says every time someone tells her they are pregnant her first thought is, *Why can't it happen to me?* Her first feeling is jealousy rather than joy for the expecting couple.

She says, "Why am I such a horrible person?" This reaction goes against everything in her make up. She is the least jealous-natured person I know and one of life's rarities that gets a great deal of joy from other people's achievements and successes. I know these feelings will pass for her, it's just because of the trauma they have been through trying to get pregnant.

I say to her, "I feel a similar way Davina. I've adopted my kids. I will never get to know what it was like to hold Rosie or Annie as babies. I know Annie was only three years old when she first came to live with us but we still won't ever get to have the bonding experience every other mother has with her baby in those early years where you hold them and cradle them and get to know them inside out. So, when I see other mothers with their babies or other mothers tell stories about their kids as babies, I wouldn't say it's jealousy I feel but there's something inside of me that feels sad and probably envious because I will never have that. I know it's not quite the same as what you are going through but I want you to know we are all human and it's probably normal to feel the way you do."

She says , "Wow I would never have thought of your situation like that or even wondered if that was something you would think about."

I reply , "Well I don't want to broadcast it, I'm trying to make you feel better."

Davina laughs, "It really has made me feel better to know you are just as twisted as me." We both laugh and continue chatting about other things. We both know it isn't funny and neither of us are twisted, it's a way of coping. We talk and then we slag each other off and then we laugh. The subject is a very delicate topic but having Davina, my person to be able to share these similar yet very different experiences with is so important. It's refreshing having such open and honest conversations with Davina. I know our stories and journeys are very different but the feelings we have in our own experiences are similar. I'm so glad to have her as my best friend. I know there is no judgement from her.

Chapter 34

The School Holidays

So, we survived the Easter Holidays, just. But now it's the first day where they go back to school and nursery and the guilt I feel is unbelievable. I have been so grumpy and short with them, especially Rosie. All she wants is to spend time with us and be around us and I couldn't have been any colder and apathetic if I tried. This is compassion fatigue at its best. I was pretty much exhausted by the constant chatter after day one and then couldn't bring it back after the sensory overload where the constant chatter invaded my brain space and I went into shutdown mode. One day she might stop trying and it will then be all my fault for being like that to her. Kit and I chatted before bed last night. We both agreed we need to try and be more tolerant of Rosie. It's easier said than done. I actually hate this part of myself. The part that can't pull it back, the part that can't be bothered, the part of me that seems uninterested. This person is alien to me. I don't understand her. I desperately want to be loving and nurturing all the time, why is it so hard for me to not consistently be the person that they need me to be? I know the answer is compassion fatigue. Rosie requires so much attention and reassurance and I get so exhausted by it. She completely floods my sensory system with incessant chatter and loudness, I end up not being able to think straight and I just snap. So many people talk about the 'mum' guilt. How you tell yourself you will do better tomorrow and then you make more mistakes the following day. This process is killing me. She's nine years old. She's had more changes in her life than I've had hot dinners. I need to be better; I need to give more. I need to be the adult that she so needs but also so deserves. I need to get rid of that silly inner child that comes out when I respond to one of her annoying behaviours. Sometimes the interactions between us is like two teenagers rather than a parent-child relationship. I need to dig deep and pull that responsible responsive adult I know is in there. I just need to work really hard. *Wait.* Just stop with these thoughts. I know I am not a mean or nasty person. I know I love Rosie and I want to do the best for her. But I also know I can't do this alone. I need help from friends and family. If I am able to share the load then my sensory system won't get so overloaded and I will be in a better position to be the best parent to Rosie. That's what I need to start doing more of.

Chapter 35

It Takes Nine Months to Grow a Baby

It's been nine months now since the girls moved in with us. I am going back to work tomorrow. I feel excited to be going back into my working role and have a purpose outside my role as mum, wife, cleaner, dog walker. It's incredible to think back to nine months ago when we were just meeting the girls.

I remember honestly thinking, *What have we done?* when we were in the transition week up north. The first night of putting Annie to bed and she kicked off big time, wrecking the bedroom, saying no to everything. Meanwhile Kit was through in the living room with Rosie playing a game and she is mouthing to Kit so the foster carer couldn't hear her, 'I hate your face'. We both left that house in stunned silence, and we never muttered the words aloud to each other, but we knew we were both thinking the same thing, *Can we do this? Can we love and parent these kids? What have we signed up to?* Don't get me wrong, sometimes I still go to bed thinking, *Can I do this? what a shit job I'm doing? I can't manage this?* But I also go to bed with my heart full of love. Love for these two complicated little beings, who have been through so much. So, when people who adopt wonder if they will instantly fall in love with their adopted child or worry if it's wrong if they don't. I would honestly say it doesn't have to be love at first sight. But the love that grows is what is special. Kids with trauma present with really difficult behaviours and those behaviours are tough. I'm not going to feel guilty for not instantly falling in love, because that's my normal. I also can't deny how hard it is but now nine months later the love is strong and grows deeper each day. It takes nine months for a baby to grow in their mother's womb. Maybe a good way to look at it as this has been the nine-month growing part of the process and now the real fun begins. Time will tell.

Chapter 36

The Change of Pace Brings New Challenges

A month has passed in our new norm.. It feels so good to say that I'm definitely not being as grumpy and short-tempered with Rosie. Being back at work has really helped with that. It has honestly been one of the best things that has happened. It feels so good to be going and being someone other than 'Mummy'. It has most definitely been a challenge getting out the door on-time to do the drop-offs and get to work on-time and then make sure I leave on-time to make sure I get to Annie before the nursery closes—there has been a few near misses! It's a whole new level of time management and organisation. Rosie has not been keen on the change of pace to morning times and I think it has been a shock to the system to see that the world doesn't revolve around her getting ready for school in the morning and now that I am getting ready and dressed for work she hasn't particularly liked the change. The second week of being back at work, I had been in work for an hour when my phone went.

"Hi Nell , don't panic…" Well understandably panic is the first thing I do. "Annie has had a fall and she's split her head open. You are going to need to come and take her to sick kids for stitches."

The poor wee soul is accident-prone—I am actually surprised that this is the first time I had to take her to sick kids since having her. She is totally reckless in her movements. What an adventure it is for her going to go to the hospital. It was all very exciting until the nurse had to rip the plaster off her head that the nursery teacher had put on.

"Ouch that hurts…" And she then continuously cries until we got out of the waiting room.

She then says , "Can you drop me back at nursery?"

I reply , "I can't, you aren't allowed to touch water or do anything that might make you bang your head for the next five days." This is not the answer she wants, which of course leads to more crying. So, I do what any semi-decent mother (who was also hungry herself) would do. I take her to McDonald's. The next four days are tough, but we do indeed manage to stop her from hitting or bumping her head again. She has lived to tell the tale. When we got home from the hospital and Rosie saw Annie's stitches, she was full of questions about what actually happened and wanted to know all the details.

She says , "Who took Annie to the hospital?"

I reply , "I did."

She says, "How could you take her; you go to work now?."

I reply, "I was at work and the nursery called me so I left straight away to get Annie."

Rosie says, "You aren't allowed to do that."

I say, "Of course I am. If anything happens to either of you, I would leave my work straight away."

She says, "Oh I didn't know that. I thought there wouldn't be anyone if you were working."

I say, "It doesn't work like that Rosie. Yes, I go to work but if either of you need me because you are hurt or ill, then I leave straight away. You both come first." I visibly see her relaxing at this newfound information. I wonder if she didn't understand the set-up because she's only been used to being with birth mum who didn't work and then being with a foster carer and looking after her was the job. She's never lived in a working family before. I notice a big difference in how she is in the mornings getting ready for school now she is more aware of the reality of a working mum. She is much more settled by the change of pace and appears much more relaxed about me going out to work. She even started telling me " I'm going to work in the hospital, Just like you when I'm older."

Annie's head has healed well, and just when she has the freedom to move around and play and splash and do as she pleases she unfortunately gets Covid. I go to collect her from nursery and she is being very grumpy and sassy, much more than normal. Now I need to clarify I did not know she had Covid and was unwell at this point. I pick her up and she looks like she has been dragged through a bush backwards. She was absolutely bogging. She tells me she took her leggings off and was just wearing her jumper as a dress. Ironically her long jumper has the word 'Happy' written over the front, but her facial expression could not be more opposite.

We are walking towards the car and she says, "I want a sweetie."

I reply, "I don't have any sweeties. You can have a snack when we get home."

A very disgruntled Annie then says, "I want a sweetie now. I'm not getting in the car." with a foot stomp and arms now folded. I open the car door and slide in the car. She doesn't budge and stands her ground. I then roll the window down and take a photo of her—she is not a happy chappy. Still not willing to budge. I then start the engine and needless to say she shot over to the car door like a rocket was shoved up her backside. She then gets in and just sobs. We get home and I then find out that Kit has tested positive for Covid she caught from a work trip abroad. Unsurprisingly, Annie then tests positive too and I realise how unwell she must has been feeling and just didn't have the vocab or know how to explain it. Instead of scooping her up I sent her into panic mode. The guilt of all guilt came creeping in! Man did I feel like the worst mother in the world. Sometimes I just get it so wrong. On the plus side the photo of her is an absolute belter. Definitely one to show when she brings someone home for the first time. Not only does Annie and Kit have Covid but I also test positive and it is the week before my marathon. I am absolutely gutted. I have trained so hard for it and now I wasn't going to be able to run it. I just can't believe it. I had managed to avoid getting Covid all this time. The day before race day I eventually test negative. I decide to run the ten kilometre with my mum so I am still taking part in one of the events. I am unbelievably exhausted afterwards. The kids run the fun run races which is great to watch them coming over the finish line and giving them big cheers. I love seeing their faces when they are so happily engaging in fun activities. I realise it's not the worst thing in the world that I didn't get to run the marathon, but I know I can't stop at this. I will have to do another marathon at a later date. Watch this space.

Chapter 37

Rugby Girl

I've just started taking Rosie to a play touch rugby on at the local rugby club that runs a Family friendly summer league for ten weeks during the summer months. She's absolutely loving it, so am I, to be honest. I played rugby for years and loved playing in the summer touch rugby tournaments. Rosie is such a competitive, determined little girl, so I thought rugby might be a good fit for her. I got her new rugby boots, shorts and a rugby top to play in . She is in her element as we turn up at the pitch side and she's all kitted out looking the part. The summer tournament is such a good set-up. We get to play together for ten weeks, a great mixture of people from seven years old right up to guys in their sixties. Rosie says "I'm going to beat you tonight Mum". I reply "in your dreams". We both laugh and she retorts "in your dreams". Rosie is in a nice mix of a team tonight and the guys are trying to set her up for a try. I have to push my competitive nature right down to my toes and allow her to run by me and score a try. She does a cartwheel to celebrate. She says " I told you Mum". "Well done, good job" and we high five. If she decides she likes it, she can join the junior team and play full contact. I'm a big fan of rugby so really hoping it's something she takes up but I'm trying to be mindful that it's my interest, so I don't want to push her into something that she's not interested in (it's so hard to stay mindful of this). We aren't able to go the following week because Kit has a work dinner and I need to be at home for Annie. . She has asked so many times "can't we just bring Annie?" I reply "no she's too little and it finishes way past her bedtime". It's a really good sign to see her so motivated to go. It's been really good for me to be going and doing this with her. It has shown me in a different light, not just the moaning mum telling her what she can do but seeing me, the person before the mum, the sporty rugby player who enjoys running around and being a team player. It has been quite a liberating process for me. So much so that it's really made me think about returning back to play for a women's team once the touch rugby family season is over. I have visions of going to watch Rosie playing her games on a Sunday morning and then she coming to watch my game on a Sunday afternoon (and then that mindful part of me says, *It's also okay if that doesn't happen and she just wants to be a dancer*).

Chapter 38

Could Have Been Awkward if He Hadn't Said Yes

It feels really good to be back at work. Now I'm back I realise just how much I missed this part of my life and how much I value my working life. It's such an important part of my identity and I'm so fortunate that I really enjoy my job and the people I work with. Most Wednesday mornings I attend a multi-disciplinary team meeting and some of my colleagues still join virtually via MS Teams (something that is now the norm since Covid). Today is the first meeting I've been along too since returning to work. I say hello and I get a warm reception and welcomed back and the consultant quickly introduces a few new faces who have joined the team in my absence. There's a new social worker, he's virtually in the meeting. He starts talking about patients and I feel like I recognise him but I just can't place how I know him. It really bothers me that I can't place him but he's so familiar. Maybe he just reminds me of someone.

The following week he comes into the office and I meet him in person.

I say , "Hello, nice to meet you in person." He starts talking and instantly I remember where I know him from. I say, "Do you sit on adoption approval panels?"

He replies , "Yes."

I say , "Oh my God you were on the approval panel to approve my wife and I do be adopters."

He says, "Oh my God, yes I remember you."

I say, "Just as well you approved me or this encounter could have been very awkward."

He laughs and says, "It's not very often people don't get approved." I instantly think back to the nerves I had before that panel and wonder why I doubt myself in these situations. It was nice to be able to tell him about the girls and the next part of our journey, although it felt really weird knowing that he has read a forty-five-page document all about me and Kit and knows every little detail of my life and now I need to work with him

Chapter 39

First Letterbox Contact

I get home from work and Kit calls me up to her office upstairs.

"The letter is here," she says.

Straight away by heart sinks a bit. The anticipation of the unsettledness this could cause Rosie fills me with anxiety. Kit had opened it and already read it.

She says , "The actual content of the letter is great."

I say, "It's the impact of receiving the letter that really worries me. Let's give her the letter straight away."

The letter is already a month late because the social services hadn't arranged the letterbox contact agreement properly. I had emailed them a few weeks ago to ask if there was a letter or not. Michelle had written the letter and posted it exactly when she was supposed to and social services then took four weeks to get things organised. Michelle had phoned three times to enquire about it. Finding this information out made me smile. I was glad to hear Michelle was still doing well and it seems like getting letters to the girls was a priority.

We call Rosie up to her room.

Kit says, "Your letter has arrived from your mum and she has sent you some photos."

Rosie takes the letter and starts looking at the photos straight away. The photos are of Michelle and Josh.

Rosie is smiling and she says, "Aw he's so cute isn't he Mum?"

Kit says, "Yeah he's really cute." Rosie then reads the letter and there is £500 worth of vouchers for her and Annie. She was absolutely delighted.

I then say, "I think you should write back straight away. Your mum has been waiting for ages to hear from you."

She replies, "Okay Mum. Can you help me?"

"Yes of course I can. Let's go out and do it in the garden while we sit in the sun." I am trying really hard to hide my apprehension and to present as relaxed and super cool. But really on the inside I have a whole mixed bag of emotions.

"How should I start my letter, Mum? Should I say Mum or Michelle?."

"Well how is your letter signed?"

"Eh, it says 'love Mum' so maybe I should say hi Mum?"

"Yes, that's a good idea."

"What should I write now?"

I say, "You can write anything you want and answer the questions that your mum asked in her letter."

She says, "Okay." And she starts to write the first line of the letter: *Hi Mum, me and Annie are really happy in our new family...* It is lucky I have my sunglasses on. I start to well up. All of my anxieties disappear instantly. Why had I been so worried about this? Right there in front of me I realise just how settled she is now. The love I feel for this beautiful perfect little person was immense. She writes such a lovely letter back where she writes about her hobbies and clubs and things she loves doing. I was fully anticipating a period of unsettledness after the letter and photo exchange but much to my surprise it never came. Don't get me wrong there has been some testing moments but not in response to her letterbox contact. I really hope the next letter comes in in November as expected. I honestly believe this is the start of the healing process for Rosie.

Chapter 40

Gay Pride March

I get a voicemail from Rosie's teacher when I am at work, It's a new teacher I haven't had much interactions with. She's now job sharing with Miss Wilson. "Hi Nell, It's Miss Smith here. I'm just wanting to give you a heads-up of something that happened in school today, it's nothing major but just wanted to explain." I am rushing out of work whilst listening to the message, thinking oh no please don't be major. I call back on handsfree whilst driving home. "I just wanted to let you know that Rosie was a little bit upset today. We were talking about Pride Month and some of the boys were being silly and not making very nice comments. Rosie got upset and took herself to the quiet corner. I have spoken with her before she left but just in case she's not okay it will be likely because of that."

"Oh, thanks so much for letting us know and thanks for openly talking about Pride Month in the classroom."

"Oh, it's my pleasure. I'm actually a bisexual myself...."

I can't even take in the rest of what she is saying because I am stuck trying to hold in my giggle at the complete overshare of the bisexual comment. I should be hanging around with those little school boys. It's times like this where my inner child rises to the surface. I finish the call, "Thank you so much, I will check in with her when I get home."

I get into the house and Rosie comes bounding downstairs in a full rainbow outfit, T-shirt with rainbow, colourful shorts and her little trainers with rainbows on them. Unbeknown to her that Miss Smith has called and told me what had happened.

"Hi darling, how was school?"

"Good. Look, do you like my outfit?"

"Yes, I love it."

"I'm wearing it to the pride March on Saturday because I want to show my support for all the gay people and help stop people from being horrible to them."

"Brilliant. The world needs more people like you." As she runs off to the back garden to go on the trampoline, I just watch her thinking, *She's going to really be someone. The world better watch out for the difference little Miss is going to make.* It is a really proud moment.

It's now Saturday and we are heading to Gay Pride March with the kids. Today is going to be very different from my Pride Marches pre-kids. We all get ready with our rainbows and face paints and go for the bus. Annie has no idea what is going on but she is delighted to be going to a 'rainbow parade'. Rosie could not have any more rainbow on if she tried. We proudly march through the centre of town. It is so busy with so many people. The Health Visitor who came to visit me a few times when the kids arrived is at the March with her Wife and little girl. I give her a wave. On the bus on the way to the march a group of people in their early twenties get on. One of them looked female but had drawn a moustache on.

Annie taps the person on the shoulder and says , "I like your moustache. Mum look do you like her moustache?."

"Yes, I love it." It's incredible to see how open and liberal kids are. There's was no judgement whatsoever. My wish in this moment is that they both keep their openness and don't allow society to change them.

After the Pride March, we go to the LGBT kids rave. Going to a rave at Pride at two p.m. and being home by five p.m. has well and truly embedded me into parenthood. The kids loved it. Gone are the days of staying out until three a.m.

Chapter 41

Nursery and P4 Come to an End

I don't think I fully appreciated how emotional I would feel when it got to the last week of Annie being at nursery. I was so caught up in thinking about how much easier it will be when I get to do the pickup and drop-off at the same place when they are both at school, I was kind of wishing nursery away… until of course I go to Annie's little nursery graduation ceremony. We all sit on the tiny little chairs and watch as each of the kids are called up from the nursery teacher to get their little graduation certificate. I am just watching her with the other kids, she is smiling and laughing and then looks over to us and waves. I can't fight back the tears. I am overcome with emotion. I can't believe how far we have come. A whole year of nursery done. She still looks so tiny and smaller than the rest of her peers. When her name is called and she walks up she is beaming with the biggest smile. My heart is bursting with pride. They all sang two songs. One of the songs is, *You Are My Sunshine.* Well, if I wasn't crying enough before I definitely let loose now. She has a beautiful little yellow sunshine dress on that my friend Davina bought her which was a perfect fit for the day. As much as I am looking forward to her starting school it is a big realisation of how quickly life can move and how fast they will grow. So much can happen in a year. The look at the difference in Rosie's first day of P4 photo compared to her last day of P4 photo is like night and day. She already looks so much older. On the last day of P4 she gets up at six a.m. and gets dressed and is sitting waiting downstairs for us to get up. I come down and ask her why she is up so early.

She replies, "You need to take my last day of P4 photo and do the comparison."

She is really overwhelmed by the whole thing. It makes me wonder how many opportunities she has had in the past where she has had a before and after of a full year in primary school and I'm not sure it has happened given her inconsistent attendance when with Michelle and then Covid-19 put the world into lockdown. A full year of 100% attendance and she absolutely loved every minute of it, even the tough moments didn't get her down. I didn't ever imagine we would have been so lucky to get such a resilient determined go-getter. She really embraces every opportunity that comes her way.

Chapter 42

A Cup of Honesty

I am meeting two of my work colleagues for a coffee this morning It's Annie's last day of nursery so I have until 11:50am. It is so great having a catch up about work stuff but also sharing stories about the kids. Frankie is thirty-two weeks pregnant with her first. It is funny listening to all the things she is doing to get prepared. It's just so different from getting ready for adoption. Lucy has two little girls, similar ages to Rosie and Annie. I really enjoy listening to her stories of her girls. For the first time I feel like my stories are quite similar and dare I say it, 'normal'. Lucy says , "Nell , I hope you don't mind me asking this and please don't feel you need to answer."

I say , "This sounds really good. Fire away." And we all giggle.

Lucy then asks , "Did you love the girls straight away?."

I instantly respond , "No I didn't. I love them with all my heart now but no I need to be honest. I didn't love them; I didn't know them. I also really didn't like the way they behaved. When I think back to the transition week where we spent the week with them with their foster carer it actually gives me nightmares."

Lucy replies , "I love how honest you are, Nell. I can totally understand why you felt that way. I've had mine from birth and when their behaviour is really bad sometimes, I really struggle but I can imagine it must be so much worse when you don't have that bond already formed."

"Yeah, that's exactly it." I then go on to tell them the story of our transition week.

It was one really tough night when we had to do bedtime routine with them during the transition week. Kit was putting Rosie to bed and I had Annie. It was horrendous. Annie did not listen to a word I asked her to do. She went totally nuts and wrecked the whole bedroom, everything she could throw went flying across the room. She would just not go to bed. She was a monster. Kit was in the living room with Rosie playing a game of cards and the foster carer was in the dining room. Rosie with her back to the foster carer mouthed to Kit, 'I hate your face'.

Kit immediately said really loudly so the foster carer could hear, "Do not speak to me like that. That is not acceptable."

Rosie straight away had a look of panic and then was stunned into silence. She was taken aback by Kit calling her out on it. Meanwhile, Annie is still going crazy in the bedroom refusing to go to bed.

Eventually after a three-hour battle, we left the foster carer's house and went back to our apartment. The silence spoke volumes. Neither of us could actually speak because if we did, we would have talked each other into not going forward with the match. It took a great deal of optimism, hope and positivity to be able to get up the next morning and go back and forget the previous night and keep going with it. I need to be totally honest I really didn't like any part of the transition week. I completely understand why it's important for the kids but by God is it tough for the adopters. Luckily a year later and there have been massive improvements in behaviour plus there is now a bond between us so it all feels more normal. We have made it very clear what is acceptable and unacceptable behaviour in our house rather than being in someone else's house who has been much more lenient.

Lucy replies , "It's so interesting listening to your stories Nell ."

I reply, "I like sharing it." It's refreshing talking to the girls about it all and looking at comparisons from then to now. It reminds me of how far we have come.

Chapter 43

Our First Family Holiday

So, our options for our first holiday are limited due to not yet having new passports for the girls. With the adoption order taking so long to come through it meant we weren't able to apply for passports until we get their new birth certificates so we have had to think creatively. I honestly would have loved to have gone on an all-inclusive holiday abroad where there was the option of kid's club and you could get a break to lie and read your book but that was not to be the case just yet. Instead, me Kit the two girls and the dog pile into the campervan and head on a trip around the NC500. Our first stop is Wick where Kit's great-aunt who is 102 years old lives. We meet Granny, Auntie Karen and their cousins Alana and Bobby on the road and spend the first few days of our holiday together. They stay at Auntie Jane's house and we book into an Airbnb apartment close by for three nights. Annie keeps asking if it is her new house and we keep reiterating that we are just on holiday. The kids love the adventure of it all, and love playing with their cousins. We go cold-water swimming, we get ice cream, we visit all the tourist attractions, we play football in the park; we sing songs and play fun games. It is a great way to start our adventure. It's day three so we pack the van, say our goodbyes and make our way along the coast to our first campsite. The weather takes a serious turn for the worse and Kit and I eventually have to give up trying to pitch the tent and we all pile into the van for the first night. It is raining so heavy and is so windy that we can feel the wind lifting the van up. Luckily, we have a DVD player in the van. It is the height of summer, but pouring rain and stuck in the van so we have to make our own indoor fun in a small space. We decide to introduce the girls to the movie *Home Alone*. Of course, Annie becomes obsessed by Kevin and all the things he gets to do to the bad guys.

It's the next morning, we all wake at the crack of dawn as we have no curtains in the van so the light comes beaming through and we are all awake before seven a.m. I go to start the engine and much to my despair the engine won't turn over. We have drained the battery by using the DVD player for so long. Thankfully, for the first time ever, I have AA cover but because we are in the middle of nowhere right at the top of Scotland, it took four hours for the mechanic to get to us. So we have no choice but to stay put on the campsite. It is still raining but the wind has died down so we get to work and put the big tent up. It is all very exciting for the girls. Once the tent is up we make some food on our little stove to kill some time and stay dry in the tent. The mechanic messages to say he is going to be delayed further so the van still can't move. We are back

I say, "Davina is your auntie. She will never take you away from your mummies. You now live with me and Mummy Kit forever. You won't have to ever find a new family ever again."

She then says, "Aww I thought I was going back to live with Freda."

I say, "No you won't ever go back to foster care."

She says, "Oh yes because you are my foster carer now."

I say, "No darling we are your family. We adopted you and Rosie to be a family with us."

"Oh okay." Off she goes skipping away to watch the TV in her pjs. It hits me like a tonne of bricks—life is still so confusing for her. Her story still doesn't quite make sense to her. She has been telling stories recently about her life as a baby. The first time we were aware of it is when she asked Kit's auntie to help her put a code in her iPad for parental controls and Kit's auntie told her that her parents need to do the code and Annie replied, "I don't have parents, they died."

Then when my mum was babysitting them, Annie told her that she had a baby sister when she was a baby and that her baby sister died in the river when she drowned. She does have quite an obsession about death and dying at the moment and this is transpiring into her own little stories. It's hard to try and understand why she is saying these things. I'm not sure she knows what parents are and because she doesn't get exact answers about when she was a baby, she is making stories up in her head to fill the blanks. It's hard for us to not overthink everything but we know we need to try and be much clearer and talk about her story to ensure she understands it and stop assuming

Chapter 44

It's Been a Whole Year

I actually can't quite believe it's been a year since the girls arrived in their new home with us. I can remember so clearly the day they came into their new house for the first time. Freda, their foster carer brought them over. They were so excited to explore every inch of their new home. Annie didn't fully understand the meaning of the whole thing but still continued to copy Rosie who was excitedly exploring every room and all around the garden. It's funny to think on that day, life was never the same again.

To mark the one-year occasion of the girls living with us we are having a BBQ party to celebrate. It is the height of the summer holidays, so a lot of friends are on holiday but we still decide to go ahead because we feel it is important to mark the year, plus Rosie is so excited to have a celebration. I feel lucky that she is so keen to celebrate that she has been adopted by us, I often wonder how much harder it could have been if it was a child who didn't have Rosie's nature and outlook on life.

The BBQ is nice and chilled and relaxed. The adults are all chatting and the kids are playing. From the outside looking in you would never tell it used to be any different. Our friends and family have brought the girls some lovely gifts. My friend Caz bought a hoody for each of us and made a print with a rainbow and put all our names on it. Rosie hadn't taken hers off all day.

We only have a few more weeks of the summer holidays left before school starts back. Rosie's been to holiday club for two weeks after our two-week holiday and Annie has been watched between us, Nana, Granny and then the last week before school my best friend Davina has been here staying and watching the girls when I am at work. Davina has been the first person out with my mum and Kit's Mum that has watched them for more than an hour or so. Davina has been great with them and they love her. Annie has been a little bit more deviant again, but no big problem for Davina to manage. I had kind of over looked what Annie would be thinking or feeling about the babysitting.

Davina leaves and I put Annie in the bath and she says to me, "Does Davina want kids?"

I reply , "Yes she does one day."

To which Annie then says , "Does she want a kid in her tummy or does she want me?." It becomes so clear to me that she has been worried that she would have to go and live with Davina now that she has been spending the last few days with her. The last time she spent time with people for a few days she then had to move in with them forever and left everything else she knew. She is confused sitting wondering if it is going to happen again.

to thinking creatively, how can we fill our day? What else is there to do when you are on a beautiful beach in the middle of nowhere? We get the girls into their wetsuits and we go swimming in the sea. We have to climb down rocks to get to the beautiful secluded beach. There is not another soul to be seen. Just us and Angus. They have such great fun but they are absolutely freezing. Angus is having the time of his life with all the humans in the water with him throwing his ball for him. We only last just under ten minutes. We then run into the campsite shower block and all have a very long hot shower before we got cosy in our tent. We make hot chocolate and play Scabby Queen continuously for two hours. The mechanic eventually turns up and it takes him all of one minute to give me a jumpstart. It has been really quite stressful and I felt like it had mucked up our plans but mainly I think about the smiles on their faces and the laughs we had today. It's moments like these that I won't forget quickly. It was intense, full-on, exhausting, but the memories made and the quality time spent together was totally worth it. We took them cold water swimming in the pouring rain in the most picturesque beach. They were fearless and always up for anything. Unfortunately, the weather didn't really improve much over the next few days as we explored other campsites. We then make our way over to the Isle of Skye and park in my Auntie Helga and Uncle Tam's drive. It is great to meet up with family again. Helga and Tam run a bed and breakfast in a big house in the countryside and my cousin Kenzie loves tractors and quad bikes and building stuff so Annie is in her element riding the tractor and investigating all the stuff on their land and in the big garage. We then take the girls to the fairy pools in Skye and we go cold water swimming. Again, it is just picturesque and so great for the girls to spend time with my auntie and uncle, they were such a big part of my childhood and I am proud to show off my girls.

After The Isle of Skye, we head to my mum's for the last few days as the weather is better the further west we go.. We spend the last few days playing in the paddling pool in the garden and relaxing. Rosie isn't quite finished with camping yet and we pitch the big tent in my mum's garden and Rosie and Abbie, the little girl who lives next door to my mum that Rosie has become friendly with both camp outside all night. She has the time of her life. Over all I would say our first holiday is a success, with a few small blips, like when Kit's Auntie Jane was helping Annie with something on her iPad a message popped up to say she needed parental guidance.

When Auntie Jane tried to explain this to Annie her response was, "Oh I don't need that, my parents are dead." Auntie Jane was stunned into silence. Kit and I reiterated that sometimes she still gets confused about it all and makes random stuff up and not to worry (some people must think we are mad by our laid-back response to these kinds of things).

Chapter 45

I Don't have a Daddy, I have Two Mummies

It's the first day of school. Primary 1 for Annie and Primary 5 for Rosie. At six a.m. they get up , they don't need to be up until seven-thirty a.m. I think it is a mixture of nerves and excitement for both of them. Annie doesn't really know what to expect and I think Rosie is a bit worried about seeing all her classmates again since she hasn't seen them all summer and she has a brand new teacher she hasn't met yet. All up and dressed in their uniforms, hair done, sparkly new shoes on and massive backpacks with nothing in them they are ready for their photographs. Their wee faces are so proud as I am taking their photos. They look so fresh and pretty. We walk along to the school the three of us hand in hand chatting and laughing. It really is lovely. We get to the playground and other P1's start to arrive with their parents. We all wait nervously for the teacher to come and call the kids in. Annie is brilliant. She is second up in the line. She runs back a few times to give me a cuddle and runs back to the line. Some kids are really crying and not letting go of their mum and dads. I really feel it for them. Annie goes in and I can see her hanging her backpack up and looking around being curious and chatting to other kids around her. I have a good feeling she is going to get on just fine. Since it is her first day, she is only in for half a day. I walk back along to collect her at lunch time. All the parents are waiting in the playground. The teacher brings the kids out in a single file line. Annie is third in the line.

The teacher starts saying to each kid, "Can you see your mum or dad?" and the kids point and then go to their parent. It comes to Annie and the teacher says, "Can you see your mum or dad? Can you point to them?."

Annie with the biggest look of disgust looks up to her teacher and says really loudly, "I don't have a dad. I have two mummies. Mummy Nell and Mummy Kit."

Of course, all eyes are on me as Annie then comes running towards me repeating, "The teacher said I have a dad but I told her I don't, I have two mummies." Being outed to all the parents on the first day of school was not what I was expecting but I guess that means there won't be any whispers of them wondering what the situation is with our family life. I have to laugh at the situation. I love how she corrects people straight away so quickly and she looks at them as if to say, 'how dare you have the audacity to make that mistake'. She makes me laugh. I'm pleased to see that she is sure of her family situation though. She's absolutely spot on, she does have two mummies and no dad and she's not in foster care and her parents aren't dead so it's a big win. She says "the first day of school was the best day ever'. I was worried we put her into school a bit too early and wondered whether we should have held her back for another year of nursery but I'm feeling confident we made the right decision now.

It's the second day of school and a card addressed to Rosie comes through the post. Kit knows it is a good luck going back to school card for Rosie from Granny but Rosie has no idea who it is from. Her face lights up when she sees she has a card. She opens the card and reads it out loud and I can see the disappointment fall all over her face.

She says , "Aww I thought that card was from the council."

To which Kit replies , "What, did you think the council were going to send you at good luck at school card?."

Rosie gives a little laugh. I am in my bedroom while they are in the hall having this conversation, I know fine well what Rosie means. She thought the card came from the council from Michelle , like letterbox contact.

I say to her later on that night, "You thought the card through the post was from your birth mum, didn't you?"

She looks up to me and says , "Yeah." And gave a little flick of her eyes.

I say , "That must have felt really disappointing darling. You will get a letter twice, one in May and one in November. I'm sure she was thinking about you on your first day."

To which she replied as she was skipping away, "Probably not." It made me realise that she will always have these little moments all through her life.

It's the following day, the three of us are in the car going down to the beach to walk Angus. .

Rosie says out of the blue, "I didn't even go to P1 and I can read." Instantly I'm thinking, *Annie starting P1 is obviously triggering for her.*

I say , "You can not only read, and write and do maths but you are also at the top of your class, which shows how determined and hard-working you are. You should feel very proud of yourself." I look in the rearview mirror and she nods and gives a little smile. Annie starting P1 must be bringing back lots of memories for her and there must be lots of comparisons going on through her head. She didn't really get the full experience of P1. It is at these times I remember that life is harder for Rosie and she has so much to contend with yet she gets up every day and strives for 'normal'.

Chapter 46

Rosie's First Rugby Training Session

It's our first Sunday morning taking Rosie to her first session with the Hawks Junior League. She is up and dressed in her full rugby kit all excited and ready to go at the crack of dawn. We all go along to watch, even Angus. . She is beyond excited. As soon as we get there and I introduce her to the coach and she gets her boots on straight away and off she goes to join in. Of course, Annie then decides she wants to play rugby too. The set-up for children is really great. Sessions run from preschool age right up to fifteen years. I take Annie up to the P1 class and she is allowed to join in. She really doesn't have a clue what she is doing. She is just running around like a crazy kid. Kit and I have to take turns on one staying with Annie and the other getting to watch Rosie. Annie needs quite a bit of parent participation to keep her engaged. My vision of standing drinking my coffee I got from McDonald's drive-through and relaxing and enjoying watching Rosie play doesn't quite match the reality of the morning. It's funny how many visions you have about things you will do as a parent and then the reality is very different. Despite the juggling of running back and forward between both the girls, I am loving it. Watching Rosie getting stuck in and seeing her being good at something and I can tell she is happy with how she is doing is so lovely to see.

The session finishes and she runs up and says, "I loved it I'm definitely coming back Mum."

I reply, "Brilliant. You were great." She is buzzing. Annie, on the other hand, leaves her session saying, "I'm maybe going to do rugby when I'm five. I'm just so tired."

I laugh, "That's a good idea."

Kit and I then split.. She takes Angus and I take the kids. We then run to the van and quickly need to get going so we can make it my friend Lizzie's wee boy's sixth birthday party. It takes an hour and half to drive there, they live where I grew up, beside my mum. The downside of living far away from where I grew up is the long drive when I go back to see family and friends. We get stuck in traffic in the city so are now short of time. I feel my stress rising. I decide to stop at a service station on the M8 and get the girls out their rugby clothes and into their party dresses in the toilets. Of course, I'm so unorganised I forgot a hairbrush and their hair is a riot. I wouldn't be surprised if people watching us thought I had kidnapped them and was trying to disguise them. We run back into the car quickly and speed off back down the M8.

Annie says, "Mummy why are we always rushing?"

I laugh and say, "Because we are a family that always try to fit too much in."

We are only fifteen minutes late to the party and I even made enough time up that I could stop quickly at my mum's to brush their hair before the party. My mum also has lovely little bows and clips to put in their hair so they really look the real deal. Never would have imagined they were unwashed and shoved in the car straight from rugby. They have a great time at the party, getting their faces painted and playing on the bouncy castle and eating all the party food. I was really relaxed too. There was no anxiety or feeling on edge wondering what they were going to do or say. It all feels so ordinary which feels incredible. A normal bog-standard mum taking her children to a party. It's a good place to be. About nine months ago, I would have dreaded this kind of situation because I would have been up to high dough about their behaviours and the things they said.

Chapter 47

The Transitions Still Causes Issues

They have been back to school for coming up to four weeks now. It's been a testing time. When things are going well, you fall into this complacency of thinking you have nailed it, that's the unsettledness gone. That is the *wrong* thing to do. It only makes the fall so much harder when you go through the unsettledness again. The first few weeks it is Rosie that is struggling. It's like she's went back 120 steps from where she had been. She is so hyperalert that she has went back to being unable to use her brain to remember important information or be at all organised. Morning routine, bedtime routine, self-care tasks—all vanished. It is like she has no head space whatsoever to function as normal. I feel like tearing my hair out. It's hard to not feel really deflated going through the unsettledness. The rational part of me knows it won't last long but the emotional, tired Nell thinks it's the end of the world. After I scrape myself up of the bathroom floor after having a quiet cry to myself, I then proceed to make some progress, or at least try. I ask Rosie to come to the dining table.

I say "What's going on with you? You really aren't yourself?"

She looks up and starts crying. We just hug for five minutes; she cries and I'm silent.

She then says without stopping for breath, "It's not fair, I want glasses. I've always been the one that wants glasses and now she's got them and everyone is saying how cute she looks and she doesn't even want them."

I'm actually gobsmacked, this is not what I was expecting to come out of her mouth. Annie got glasses after we went to the opticians two weeks ago. Rosie was told she has twenty-twenty vision.

I say without thinking, "You can't be serious? It's a good thing you don't need glasses." This comment is obviously not helpful and not what she wants to hear. I then continue, "There's lots of things you have that Annie doesn't have."

"Like what?" she replies.

"Like you have beautiful straight hair, she's got curly hair, you have an iPad and she doesn't. It's normal to feel a bit jealous but I promise you, you have nothing to be jealous of. You have twenty-twenty vision. You can do any job in the whole wide world. A pilot if you want. Annie can't because of her eyesight." Rosie then gives a little laugh. I then say, "Is anything else bothering you at school?." She then opens up and goes on to tell me that the wee boy beside her is annoying her and getting the rest of the table involved in trying to annoy her. When she puts things out on her table, he then moves them and hides them. The thing that upset her most was when she got up put her seat to get something he moved her seat away and she went to sit back down and fell on the floor and everyone laughed. She says she didn't tell on him because she doesn't want the rest of the class to be annoyed at her. I say , "It's not okay for him to be trying to make a fool out of you by doing that. He's being a bully and targeting you. I want to phone the school to talk to your teacher about this."

"No Mum, don't, you don't have to, I don't want you to."

I say , "Rosie I as your mum can't just sit and not do anything about this. It's my job to make sure you are okay, so I have to phone the school."

She smiles and says , "Okay Mum."

I speak with the class teacher the following day who is absolutely brilliant. It's my first dealing with her new teacher now she's in P5 and I am delighted with the response. Mrs Jamieson , is going to do a change up of all the seats the next day and make sure she separates them and does it discreetly. She asks who Rosie gets on with and I tell her the two girls she likes. Mrs Jamieson is going to sit Rosie next to one of them. I don't tell Rosie what Mrs Jamieson is going to do. I just tell her that the wee boy will be told he can't do that to her or other kids.

The next day she comes running back from school. "Mum, Mum, guess what? We all got moved seats and I'm beside Amanda and Jack is all the way at the other side of the class."

I say , "Oh brilliant, that's lucky."

And she replies , "I know." With a happy shocked expression. As she runs into the house, I watch her with a little smile. I am now feeling hopeful there might be a difference now she has a better table in school.

Not long after Rosie settles in her behaviour, Annie then starts. It's unbelievable! It's like they tell each other to have a go so we can drive the parents crazy. Annie starts wetting the bed most nights or if she doesn't pee the bed, she gets out the bed and pees on the rug beside her bed. It's absolutely exhausting constantly washing the sheets and scrubbing the rug. I just get so frustrated by it. I'm like is she actually doing it 'cause she's lazy? Can she not help it? Is she not going to the toilet enough during the day? She is also not wanting to wipe her bottom when she has a poo and I just don't get it.

I am like sixty seconds late to pick her up from school today and boy oh boy do I pay the price. She cries so hard, absolutely sobbing when we got home.

She keeps saying, "I miss Freda. I miss foster care." It absolutely pierces through my heart having to listen to her say these things. It makes me question everything. *Doesn't she feel loved? Are we being too hard on her? Is it so much harder for her here that it was in foster care?* The guilt is unreal. I try to find out more how she's feeling.

I say, "Do you miss Freda's house?"

She replies, "I don't know what her house looks like?"

I say, "Do you miss Freda's cuddles?"

She says, "What does Freda look like?" I then start to realise it isn't Freda she misses. It's been such a long time since she seen Freda. It's the not knowing that makes her sad and unsure. All her new friends in school will all have stories and she can't remember hers. I instantly feel flooded with sadness for her. She is experiencing a great deal of loss and uncertainty and unable to process it for it to make sense.

I say, "Why don't we get your special book and look at your baby pictures and there will be Freda and your birth mum."

She replies, "I don't want to see them, I want sweeties."

I laugh and say, "Why don't you have some sweeties and look at your special book at the same time?"

She replies, "Oh okay then."

I get her some skittles and get her special book. I start going through the book and showing her baby photos. She loses interest straight away.

"Mum can I just go on the iPad?" I say yes and let her sit and relax. I decide I don't want to force her. All the information is there when she wants it.

After sitting on the iPad for five minutes she looks up and shouts, "Mum will you never leave me because I'm too precious?" Her question hit me like a bus.

"I will never leave you. You are the most precious girl." I then follow on with, "Do you worry you will be left?"

She says , "No I don't worry." But I think by the questions it was quite obvious this is where the meltdown came from. I went over to her and cuddle her so tight. I just sit for a while, holding her, hoping that she will one day believe she is safe and loved forever.

After a few weeks, thankfully the bedwetting stops , it must have been related to all the big changes with going to school and trying to process her little life. The wiping of her bottom is still an ongoing battle, but I suppose I can't win them all.

Chapter 48

Please Sir Can I have Some More

Kit comes back from the park and says, "Annie was talking to some older kids at the park. They knew who she was because she has been going to their playground and asking for food during play time."

I reply to say, "That's interesting, I've just had an email from her teacher telling me the exact same thing." As I'm talking Annie hides at the other side of the dining table looking a bit embarrassed.

I continue to speak, "You have your own play piece Annie; you don't have to go and ask other people for theirs."

She pops her head round from behind the chair and says, "But they have better things than me."

I say, "What have they got that you want?"

She replies, "Cheese string, crisps, chocolate."

I say, "I can get you cheese strings and you can have that with your banana or apple but you have to stop taking other kids' snacks."

She looks at me with those big brown eyes. "Okay Mum."

I'm not convinced she isn't going to go into school again tomorrow and keep asking but time will tell. I think this is going to be gentle reminders to steer her away from doing it. It surprises me that she is doing it. I didn't expect Annie to have any issues with food because she was taken into foster care at such a young age but we have had a few issues related to foods. When we go to parties she goes absolutely crazy and eats so much that she ends up feeling sick. It's like she needs to eat as much as she can fit in in case she doesn't ever get the chance to eat again. We have a fifth birthday party planned for Annie next week at the house and the thing she is most excited about is eating the food.

Chapter 49

She's Not the Bloody Queen

We have the first 'share your learning' of the year at school for both girls.. Only one parent per child can attend. Kit goes to Rosie's and I go to Annie's... It is so good to see all the little bits of work Annie is doing in class. She is so proud showing all her work. Her teacher says she is a pleasure to have in the class, she's always so enthusiastic about everything they do and always has a positive can-do attitude. I feel very proud.

She looks up at me and says with the straightest face, "Mum I have been very busy at school and that's why I'm so hausted."

She means exhausted of course. She sounds like a wee granny.

I laugh and she continues, "It's not funny Mum."

I say, "Sorry I didn't mean to laugh; I do understand just how tired you must be after seeing all your hard work."

"Yes," she says. The teacher calls the kids to let them know they need to head back to class and to say bye to their parents.

I say, "Thanks for showing me all your work, you are doing amazing."

She replies, "I know Mum. Bye." I head off to my work feeling a sense of pride and happiness.

Later that night, Kit tells me Rosie's work is really great too and she was beyond excited to show off to Kit. Something she hasn't done for a while is use a baby voice and Kit said she had to tell her a few times to not use her baby voice during her visit to see her school work. Kit isn't really sure why she fell back into the habit of using it but because she hasn't done it for a while and then did it in front of her peers and their parents Kit felt that original embarrassment we contended with when we first were dealing with behaviours in public. Talking about embarrassment; the day before the sharing your learning visit, I am standing in the playground dropping Annie to school with Rosie beside me. They go in at separate times and in different playgrounds.

I see the headteacher walking with a few other teachers and I say to Rosie, "Run up and ask Mrs Dickie what time the sharing your learning is happening." I stupidly sent the signed slip back and didn't note the time, only the date. So, Rosie runs up to Mrs Dickie and I see her waiting politely for her to stop speaking to other teachers before she asks her about the time. Mrs Dickie doesn't realise I am standing behind and assumes Rosie is on her own. I can't quite make out what she is saying to Rosie but I can see Rosie's face getting red and she is obviously getting embarrassed. I start to walk over and I hear her say in a condescending unhelpful tone, "All the information is on the app, I'm not going to run around finding out the specific details for your mum."

Rosie doesn't know what to say so just stands there and glances at me approaching. I am feeling rage build inside me. I have seen the headteacher speak really condescendingly to Annie's class teacher when we went for the transition afternoon and I didn't warm to her then, but now I've seen her speak like this to Rosie the fury inside me has went from one to 100.

I march up and say, "Come on Rosie maybe the office staff might be a bit more bloody helpful." Mrs Dickie looks round, completely surprised of by presence. I march forward with Rosie half running to keep up with me.

She says, "Mum, Mum, that's Mrs Dickie, she's the headteacher."

I reply, "I don't care who she is, she's not speaking to you like that. She's not the bloody queen."

Rosie is utterly mortified, but remains silent. I go into the school office and they are much more helpful and they confirm that the times have not been uploaded onto the app.

I say, "Are you able to tell the headteacher that before she decides to embarrass another child for asking a reasonable question?" The office lady doesn't quite know how to respond.

She half-smiles and replies awkwardly , "Yes of course. I will update the app." Probably if I hadn't been on my period, I wouldn't have been so reactive. But in a way,

I'm glad it happened the way it did. I was glad for Rosie to see that I will stick up for her and it doesn't matter who you are you should speak to everyone with common courtesy and respect. When I drive off to work the realisation hit me that this is probably the first time since coming to live with us that it is Rosie who is embarrassed by me in public rather than the other way round. I feel like I reached a milestone. My rage subsides and I happily go into work to share the story with my colleagues. It is funny talking about it to my colleagues who are also parents.

Liz, parent of two kids says , "Isn't it funny how you become so much more assertive when it's your kids you're sticking up for?." It was like a light-bulb moment. She is right. I probably would never have had that reaction if it had just been me but because she done it to Rosie it was a completely different story. Is it new found assertion, or am I just a grumpy Mother on her period? Probably a bit of both.

Chapter 50

Annie Turns Five

We have a birthday party at the house for Annie's fifth birthday. This year we decide to invite more people and it is much busier. It's funny when I think back to how I felt at her fourth birthday party when she had only been with us for two months. I was a nervous wreck having that party. I honestly had no idea how she would cope or what her behaviours would be like. Now I feel like I can predict how she will behave and I feel much more settled myself. I was happy to have our house full of family and friends and I wasn't on edge. What a difference a year makes. Even comparing how Rosie copes compared to last year is like night and day. She obviously isn't feeling as threatened by Annie getting attention and she even appears to be enjoying herself much more. We play lots of party games and have the neighbours and their kids as well as family and friends this year.. The only thing we have to keep an eye on is Annie not eating too much of the party food. She has to be redirected away from the table a few times. The good thing is that she is accepting of the redirection and off she goes to play with the other children. Davina, Lizzie and Cat all made the journey through with their kids, their kids all have lovely brushed hair and hadn't been quickly changed in a service station on the journey over. I love seeing Annie spending time with and playing with them. The four of us have been best friends since we were fifteen. We call our little group 'Palchat' and we now call the kids 'Palchat juniors'. Palchat Juniors are having a ball playing together at the party. It makes my heart happy just watching.

Chapter 51

All Aboard

The girls' passports finally come through after several months of waiting. We are desperate to book a sunshine holiday so we book to go to Tenerife for the October break. It is a four-star all-inclusive, and it is absolutely brilliant. We have great weather all week which really helps.. The kids are just unbelievably excited, especially Annie. Rosie moves between being excited to feeling mixed about it. Rosie has been to Disney Land Paris and to Greece with her birth mum when she was little. Annie went too but she can't remember. We are in the airport sitting eating lunch before heading to the gate. Two women with dark hair in their early twenties sit at the table next to us and Annie shouts at the top of her voice whilst pointing right to them, "Mum that's my mother who took care of me when I was a baby but couldn't handle me."

I am literally like, *What the actual f*ck, where on earth has this come from.* The women just look at us awkwardly and smile.

I say , "No Annie that's not your birth mum, that looks like her but it's not her."

Rosie is looking super cagey. I instantly know she has been doing small whispers in Annie's ears about birth mum. No one has ever used the phrase 'couldn't handle you' so straight away I think, *has this come from Rosie?* I don't make an issue of it and we just move on from it. Kit missed the whole thing because she was at the shop. Her face is a picture when I quietly update her when she returns.

The holiday overall is really great. We teach Annie how to swim and she went from having to wear her life jacket only being in the baby pool to swimming around like a little dolphin with no life jacket and able to go into the deep pool. This was a hard pill to swallow for Rosie. She didn't learn to swim until she was eight. I quickly act and decide to take her to the deep pool and teach her how to dive which she learns really quickly and is really good. They both have learned something different and get praise for it. It's such a shame Rosie is so jealous of her sister. But also amazing she is able to verbalise it.

Rosie talks a lot about her birth mum whilst we are on holiday. It's the most she has really spoken about it. I think going on holiday with her birth mum was one of her fondest memories and it was really good time for her. Understandably I can see why being on holiday would remind her of the good times with birth mum and make her feel a bit sad.

I say , "Do you feel a bit sad and miss your birth mum?"

She replies , "No I don't feel sad because of that. I feel sad because Annie gets more attention than me."

I think she definitely does feel sad because she perceives Annie gets more attention but I think, she's also experiencing loss and grieving.

She eventually says , "I get mad because Annie can't remember, it's not fair."

I say , "I can understand how that can be frustrating for you, but it's not Annie's fault."

I think the holiday was probably most difficult for Rosie to navigate through and she could see everyone else was relaxed and enjoying themselves, especially Annie and I think that makes Rosie feel worse because she so desperately strives to feel happy and 'normal' and sometimes can't comprehend herself why she feels sad or on edge. Despite this they both play well with all the kids at the swimming pool and are in their element at the kids disco every night. They get up to dance every night. This is the most relaxing part of the day. We get to sit and sip on our ice-cold beer and watch the children's entertainer deal with the kids for forty uninterrupted minutes. It is bliss.

We are delayed in the airport on the way home. I give Rosie three euros to spend in the shop and tell her whatever she gets she needs to share with Annie. She spends one hour and ten minutes in the same shop unable to decide what to get. Eventually our gate is called and I run over to get her.

I shout, "Hurry our gate is up."

She replies, "Oh I just can't decide, I really don't want to share with Annie."

I shout, "Whatever you get Annie gets half."

She picks up these spicy crisps and decides to buy them. I am watching her and I know exactly what she's thinking. She thinks Annie doesn't like spicy crisps so she can have the lot.

She then pays and comes out and I say, "Why did you buy spicy crisps?" She looks up at me knowing fine well I have caught her out.

She says straight away, "Because I know Annie won't eat spicy crisps." I feel so mad at her for doing this. The time she spent in that shop making sure she got something that she wouldn't have to share. I just shake my head at her. She knows fine well I'm not happy. Kit and Annie are at the gate waiting.

Annie says, "What did you get Rosie?"

Rosie replies, "Spicy crisps, but you won't like them."

Surprisingly Annie says, "I want to try them." Rosie's face drops.

I say, "Give your sister the crisps." Much to my enjoyment Annie decides she now likes spicy crisps.

"Oh, I like spicy now," she says. Rosie looks like she's just received the most devasting news in the world.

I say, "Annie have as much crisps as you want." Rosie is absolutely furious.

I then say, "Maybe next time when you are told to get something for you both to share you won't take over an hour trying to work out what to get that Annie won't like." She just stares at me furiously. I can't believe this is the time Annie now decides she likes spicy. The timing is perfect. Hopefully that will be a lesson she won't forget.

Chapter 52

The Unexpected Chats

We get home from the airport at two a.m. and it's all straight to bed, Annie feels sick from exhaustion. As soon as everyone is awake on Saturday morning, we all head to Nana's to pick up our handsome boy Angus. My mum's wee dog, Bonny , has also just had a litter of puppies so Annie is beside herself to go and see tiny puppies. Angus is delighted to see us when we arrive to pick him up. There's probably a part of him that was hoping it was just Kit and me. It must be hard for him from going to our prized little prince to now being third in the pecking order. We are staying over at my mum's for the night. She takes Rosie out to the shops with her and Kit and I chill with Annie in the house. They are away for a good few hours and we enjoy the quiet time with Netflix on and Annie playing with the millions of toys my mum has collected over the years. When Mum gets back she tells me that Rosie had a wee heart-to-heart with her.
She says , "Rosie started talking about her birth mum."

I say, "Yeah, she has spoken a lot about Michelle when we were on holiday. Being on holiday obviously made her think about her last holiday with her mum."

Mum says, "She told me her and Annie can't go back and live with her because she can't handle us."

I say, "That's where Annie got that expression from, we have never used that expression before, so it makes sense now." I say, "I'm going to take her for a dog walk with Angus around the park and see if she wants to chat about anything if she's just with me."

We get our waterproofs and wellies on. The weather is nothing like the glorious sunshine we had in Tenerife. We are walking in the park and I say, "Was it hard for you being on holiday?"

She says, "No, why?"

I say, "The last holiday you went abroad it was with your birth mum, so I just wondered if it brought back memories and maybe made you feel sad?"

She says, "No I'm not sad, but I definitely think I've been to Tenerife before."

I say, "No it was Greece you went to, it might have felt similar, but it wasn't the same."

She then continues, "It's annoying that Annie can't remember. She has already been on a plane and went on holiday but she is acting like she hasn't."

I say, "She isn't acting, she can't remember, she was only a tiny baby."

She then says, "She can't remember anything."

I then say, "I think that might have been hard for you when we were on holiday because you probably really noticed it. She can't even remember being in foster care, she can only remember being here. We need to tell her story of her past."

She says, "Yeah I just won't talk about it with her."

I say, "It's okay to talk about it with her but you just have to be aware her experiences are completely different from yours."

She says, "It's not fair."

I say, "I know."

She then says, "Will I go back to see my birth mum?"

And I say, "Yes you probably will when the time is right for you."

She says, "Will I get another letter?"

I say, "Yes you are due your letterbox contact next month. I will be nice for you to be able to write to your birth mum and tell her everything you have been doing, you have been very busy."

She says, "Yeah I guess." She then says, "Mum can you tell me why you adopted me? Like, how did we end up with you?"

I say, "You want to know the process we went through?"

She says, "Yeah the process, like from the start to the finish." I then start telling her about the process starting right from the beginning.

She then says, "But how did you pick us, why me?"

I then say , "It's hard to explain, it's a gut feeling. I clicked into your information and there was a short video of you playing a tune on the piano and then you were drawing a love heart and you said to the foster carer 'this is for your family' and I was instantly completely taken by you. I said then when I found out more about you, I just needed to know more and more."

She smiled and then says , "And what did you find out about me?"

I reply , "I got to know most of your story, well as much as social work knew. I was told about all the hard and tough times and I was told how amazing you are and how much you love Annie." She is quietly listening to every word I say. I continue , "But what really sealed the deal for me was when I met your birth mum"

She looks up amazed and confused. "Why?"

I say , "Because I liked her. She was honest about how many mistakes she had made and how she wished she had done better. She was warm and open when she met with us. Mummy Kit really liked her too. I really got the sense that she really loved you but she just didn't have the skills or the right support around her to make it good enough for you and Annie. I know there are things that have happened that made you feel unsafe and that makes me sad. Your birth mum said, 'All I want is for them is to be loved and safe.' I knew right at that moment I wanted you in my life so I could love you and keep you safe and try and give you as many opportunities as possible to give you a good childhood with good memories. And then maybe when you're an adult you might decide to keep me in your life 'cause we had good times together in your childhood."

She then put her arms around my waist and says , "You will always be in my life, you're my mum."

I smile down at her and say , "We were never going to try and replace your birth mum and we never will."

"I know." She looks up.

I then say, "And when the time is right, you can reconnect with your birth mum again."

"Yes, I know that now," she says.

We then go on to chat about other random things and the conversation is closed. It reminds me of how much she has to think about and what is going on in her head. The four-and-a-half-year age difference is really tough and really highlights the differences they are experiencing. I think to myself, *I just need to keep the line of communication open and hopefully she knows she can continue to come to us when she's navigating through difficult feelings.*

Chapter 53

The Playground Kiss

I'm sitting typing on my laptop in the front room and Annie is in the kitchen playing on her iPad. Rosie then comes bursting in from school like a hurricane.

"Annie, Annie, I'm your sister, I love you, do you love me? Kiss me, kiss me."

Annie immediately shouts, "Go away Rosie." I know for certain that something has happened at school that has made Rosie come home and be as intense as this.

She pops her head into the front room. "Hi Mum, guess what? The architect for the new school came and we got to give ideas and I…" She went on for about two minutes without stopping. Her eyes wide and her body rigid.

I then say, "Rosie what has happened at school?"

"Nothing, why?"

"The way you came storming in and what you said to Annie is not how you normally greet people."

Then she burst out, "A boy called Germany kissed Annie at playtime, the boys in my class told me."

I would never have guessed that's what was going to come out her mouth. I let out a little half laugh, partly at the situation and partly because I was pretty certain there wasn't a boy called Germany in Annie's class and he's actually called Jeremy.

She then continues, "She's not old enough."

I say, "Why are you this upset about this?"

And she replies in the most honest way, "Because no one is trying to kiss me." I close my laptop.

"Rosie, just because a wee boy tried to kiss Annie does not mean people wouldn't want to kiss you or Annie doesn't love or need you any more. It's doesn't mean anything about you. You are beautiful and plenty people will want to kiss you. This is not something you need to be jealous of. This doesn't mean Annie is more beautiful or you are any less than her. They were probably playing tag and it's really innocent."

She says, "Yeah I guess so."

I then say, "Now I don't want you thinking you need to go into school tomorrow and try and kiss a boy thinking you need to get one up on this." Her little face drops . I continue, "Have you already done this?"

"Yes, but he wouldn't kiss me." I want to put my hands on my head but I'm trying really hard to respond in the best way.

"Rosie, you honestly don't need to do that. What difference would it have made if you had kissed a boy today? You don't need to go chasing boys to kiss you. I'm telling you; you are beautiful and when the time is right you will have plenty of options. You don't need to be the girl that tries to chase the boys for a kiss. Trust me."

"Okay Mum I won't do that again."

I say, "I know you felt really really jealous today and that's why you then went a wee bit crazy." She let out a little laugh. I continue , "It's really normal to feel jealous, even as an adult I need to work on how I need to hide my jealousy and respond in a good way to situations. It takes practice."

"I really need to practice," she says.

I follow on with, "And if the boys in your class see how much it annoys you they will keep goading you about it."

"Yeah, they kept going on about it and laughing."

"Yeah, because you were giving them a response." We then go on to practice 'laughing it off' scenarios. I am playing the role of Rosie to show her what she should do then I am being the wee boy. Kit is upstairs in her office working and has no idea of the kissing situation but can hear me role playing the scenarios. She must be thinking, *What on earth is she up to now.*

Chapter 54

The Big Performance

Rosie has her first dance show performance this weekend. The lead up to the show has been traumatic, mainly for me. I dropped her off to a full day of rehearsals a week before the show and I wasn't organised and she told me at the last minute that she needs to pay £5 for the day. I only had a £20 note and she needed a fiver plus lunch.

I say, "I will take you to home bargains which is right next door to the dance school and you can grab a sandwich and split the £20 to take a fiver."

"Okay Mum, good idea."

"Fill your drink bottle and take that with you please."

"Okay Mum, I've done it." I park outside home bargains and she's got eleven minutes before her rehearsal starts.

I say, "Nip in quickly and run out with my change." I sit in the car for what feels like forever.

It's now 11.01 a.m. She's been in there twelve minutes. She then appears at the car door, crying, "There's not a sandwich that I like."

I say, "Right come on there will be something in Aldi." We go into Aldi and she picks a cheese and pepperoni roll. She's happy again, but still, she's now over five minutes late. I say, "where's your drinks bottle?"

"Oh, I left it in the car." I press the car to unlock and tell her to run over and get it. She's ages looking all around the seat then she looks up and the tears come again, "I left my bottle in the house."

I'm thinking *Oh my God this girl is a riot*. "Right, you have your fiver and here's the change, there's like £2.27 use this to nip over to home bargains on your break and get a drink then."

"Can I use the money for a drink and a sweet?"

"Yes, but make sure you get a drink." She appears delighted at this concept of getting to go over and buy her own drink at break.

"Now please Rosie, remember and find out about what costumes you need, what you need to wear on your feet, what your hair has to be like and any other important details, we only have a week left before your show."

"Okay Mum, can I get fizzy sweets?"

"Rosie, have you listened to what I've just asked you, it's important for your show?"

"Yes, Mum I know."

"Okay hurry in now. Bye." She runs on in. Honestly her head is in the clouds. I'm hopeful she has listened and will find out the information. I've never been a dancer so have no idea about what she will need so I'm relying on her to get me the information.

The day passes by and I go and collect her at the end of the day. She comes running to the car. No hello or any greeting she goes straight into telling me exactly what juice and sweets she bought at break time. I say, "Did you find out about costumes and everything you need?"

Her face drops. "Oh, I forgot. But it's okay the information is all on the app." We get home and I check the app. The dance teacher has put a run through of all the dances in order of the show and what costumes are provided and what dancers need to purchase themselves.

I say, "Okay Rosie tell me which dances you are doing?" I give her the list.

She reads it for ages, constantly scanning she then looks up and says, "I don't know which ones I'm doing."

I reply, "Are you kidding? What are you practicing every week?"

She says, "Well I think I'm doing that and that." Pointing at the list. Meanwhile an email comes through from the dance teacher saying she is no longer taking phone calls and all the information has been provided in the app. The show is on Saturday and it's Monday. Her last rehearsal is on Friday. I can just see me running around trying to find dance stuff and not have a clue what I'm looking for at the last minute. The anxiety I have over this whole dance shows is through the roof. I really hope she knows what she's doing on the day and they keep her right. A meltdown on the day is the last thing she needs.

I get in from work on Friday and she comes running up to me.

"I know all the dances I'm doing and I have all my costumes and everything I need I already have." I feel relieved I don't have to go on a mad dash for anything.

I then say, "What time have we to drop you off at?"

She says, "Aw I don't know that."

I half-laugh and say, "Okay, well we will drop you early to be on the safe side." Kit is exasperated when I get home. Friday is my only long day at work and Kit has been trying to work whilst watching Annie on a Friday afternoon whilst Rosie goes to musical theatre and Annie is at the age that she can now join musical theatre too but we wanted to wait until Rosie got the chance to perform her dance show first so it could be her thing on her own without having to compete with Annie. The sooner they both go the better it will be for Kit.

She says , "Can we just go out for dinner? Annie has decided to paint her own unicorn in her school uniform and got it everywhere." The good thing is she named it Rosie Possie and had a great time.

It's the morning of the show and Rosie is super excited. I'm a mixed bag, I'm really nervous as I so badly want it all to go well. I have this vision of the kids being on stage performing and Rosie being behind stage, lost in her own wee world missing out on her performance and then being devastated. I wish I felt more relaxed about it. I sometimes think about the 'old Nell' the 'childless Nell' and I miss how much more chilled out and relaxed I used to be. I've got my game face on and as far as Rosie knows I'm as cool as a cucumber and nothing but excited to see her perform. She gets her hair put up in a bun and she needs to put make-up on which she is beyond chuffed about. I tell her to close her eyes as I apply eye shadow. She has the most beautiful long eyelashes. She has no idea just how beautiful she is. I then apply her blush and put on mascara—not that she needs it but she desperately wants it on. She looks perfect, the most perfect delicate little dancer. Our family and friends start to arrive. My best pal Davina and her husband Conrad arrive along with my mum. They make a big fuss of how good she looks. She looks so happy, it's so nice to see. Kit takes her down to the theatre so she's there before everyone else and is ready. I'm still feeling so anxious. My brother then phones to say they are stuck in traffic so will meet us there and Kit's family are in heavy traffic too. This is making me even more nervous. Of course, It was all unnecessary worrying because of course everyone gets there on-time and we are all seated for the show starting.

So, I don't have a clue really what dances she is doing but I have heard her playing several of the same songs on her Alexa in her bedroom so have a fair idea what to look out for. The opening song is the *Greatest Showman.* I have heard this song so many times so I'm anticipating seeing her. I'm clapping as the dancers come on at different times and I wait and wait but Rosie doesn't come on. My heart sinks. Where the hell is she? I'm trying my hardest to look relaxed to everyone else. Rosie then comes on stage after about thirty minutes in. She has the biggest smile on her face and she absolutely owns it. She knows every step and every move. Annie is shouting like crazy for her and she hears her and smiles even more. My heart is bursting with pride. I'm woo wooing and clapping and suddenly feel the tears running down my face. She is a shining star. All the worry and anxiety were worth it. I finally start to relax and I enjoy every single minute of watching her perform. At the end of the show, we all give a standing ovation and I shout, "we love you Rosie." Her smile is so wide.

We all wait for her to come out in the lobby. Granny has flowers for her and I watch all our friends and family hug her and tell her how amazing she was. I then give her a big hug and say, "I'm so proud of you, you were incredible."

She says, "Mum you were so embarrassing shouting at me."

I laugh and say , "That's what mums do." Secretly I know she is chuffed to bits and wasn't at all embarrassed. She has another show this evening too so she has to go back straight away. We all go back to the house and order Chinese. I feel an immense sense of pride, not just about Rosie but Annie too. The whole day she was so excited to see her big sister perform on stage and she was clapping and cheering and shouting her name so loud and although Rosie didn't say it, I know deep down that would have meant so much to her. As I am dishing out the Chinese food to our friends and family back at the house I hear Annie say to her cousins "Aren't my mummies so nice giving us all this food?" She doesn't understand that we haven't actually paid for it all. She obviously is feeling a sense of pride herself.

Chapter 55

Halloween… Nailed It!

It's Halloween. Trying to keep them entertained after school and stop them getting their Halloween costumes on too early has been a difficult task. The excitement is just too much for them. We have an early dinner and Annie is faffing about not really eating her fish fingers.

I say, "If you can't eat your fish fingers then you won't be able to eat any sweeties you get from trick-or-treating. She looks up. "I am eating my fish fingers; I'm just taking my time," she replies. Sure enough, she clears the plate clean. "Look Mum, I can now eat all the sweeties."

Rosie dresses up as Harry Potter and Annie has a dinosaur costume.

Annie keeps saying, "Mum am I going to look really scary?"

I say, "Yeah terrifying." But in reality, she's far from it. She's just so cute. When she runs around the dinosaur tale waggles from side to side. I get the face paints out and I paint her whole face green. I then go to help Rosie with her hair and come back and Annie has bright-red lips.

She says, "Look I had to make me more scary and do red lips."

I say, "Oh yeah." Half-laughing. We arranged to go guising with the neighbours and their kids. The number of sweeties they get is unreal. Kit is away over night for work so it's just me and the girls.

Once we have finished guising I say, "Right we need to take Angus a walk before we get ready for bed." They are both quite happy to do this, especially Annie who is buzzing from her sugar rush after pocket munching the whole way round the estate. We then get in out from the cold and they both get ready for bed really easily and there's no big meltdowns and no fighting, I was not anticipating it to be this easy. I think back to last Halloween and I realise how much more relaxed I am and how they both managed and enjoyed it so much more. Annie had the biggest meltdown last year when trying to get her to bed after guising. I remember last year being nervous because I didn't really know how it all works with taking kids trick-or-treating and this year I had my little gang of mum friends with their younger kids taking them guising for the first time and I was no longer the novice. They were looking to me as having the low-down on how it all works. I make a cup of tea, steal some chocolate from their buckets and I'm feeling good. Reflecting on the difference from last year, I realise just how different it is. Not just their behaviour but how I am different. I'm not as anxious or nervous. I looked forward to it. I say out loud to myself, "You owned it tonight Nell." Angus snuggles in on the couch and I watch *Grey's Anatomy* before going up to bed. It's been a good day.

Chapter 56

My Godfather Moment

It's Tuesday, the busiest day of my week. As soon as I finish work I rush to the school to pick up Annie, quickly get her home and into her swimming stuff, pick up Rosie's bag and rush back to the school to pick up Rosie for the swimming lessons. Every week I say to Rosie, "Get straight out as soon as the bell goes. We can't be late for Annie's lesson."

I'm parked at the front of the school, bang on-time for pick up at 3.10 p.m. Kids are pouring out from the front gate. 3.11 p.m. no Rosie yet, there's still some stragglers. 3.14 p.m. I can see a few kids gathering on the inside of the gate. I get out the car and can see Rosie in the middle of it.

I shout, "Rosie hurry up please." She turns and she looks frantic.

She comes running up, "Someone has stolen my scooter. I parked it right there at the end point with all the other bikes and now it's gone."

I say, "Was it locked?"

She replies, "No I never lock it because I don't have a lock."

I say, "Maybe someone has just taken a shot of it and will put it back, we will check after swimming. Come on we need to go now." She is completely silent in the car on the way to swimming.

She then says, "Do you know why I'm so sad about my scooter getting stolen?"

I say, "I think I know; it's because it was a present from your birth mum." She nods as her eyes fill up. I say, "Listen it might be back when we go and check after swimming and if it isn't then I will report it stolen to the police."

She says, "Okay."

I then say, "Are you absolutely certain you took it to school this morning?"

She replies, "Yes I did and I remember parking it in the end bit of the bike rack and talking to my friends as I put it there." We get to the swimming pool and luckily this week she has remembered her swimming costume so can actually take part in her lesson, unlike when Kit took her last week she brought everything but her costume so couldn't do her lesson. After the lessons it's always a mad dash to quickly get changed to get back for brownies and so we don't get stuck in the bad traffic. We quickly stop outside the school to double-check the scooter hasn't been put back but as expected, there is no scooter.

I say, "Right I will phone and report it missing, you just never know."

She then says, "If I don't get it back then I'm asking Santa for a new scooter and a lock." We get back to the house and she needs to have her dinner and gets her Halloween costume on for her party she is having at brownies. I'm feeling exhausted. It's nearly eight p.m. and it has been nonstop since my alarm went off at seven-fifteen this morning. I'm completing my last chore of the day. I open the back door to take the bin out and as I step out, I trip over some obstruction on the ground between the door and the wheelie bin. I don't believe what I'm seeing. It's the goddamn scooter. It hasn't left the garden. She didn't take it to school. I shout on Kit and Annie and tell them to close their eyes and watch me. I get on the scooter and start scooting around the back garden in my pjs and dressing gown.

Annie says, "Oh someone brought the scooter back."

I laugh and say, "No! Your sister didn't take it to school. It wasn't stolen, it never left the garden."

I say to Kit, "Honestly, that girl is a nightmare." I then say, "Let's put her scooter under her duvet in her bed for her to find there. I need to get some kinda laugh from this." Annie thinks it's the funniest thing ever. Rosie gets back from brownies and seems quite happy, really enjoyed her party and doesn't mention the scooter.

I say, "The police wanted me to double-check where exactly you left your scooter, Rosie?."

She replies, "Oh I definitely left it at the bike rack in the last slot."

And I say, "Are you definitely sure of that?"

She replies, "Yes, I remember everything. I was talking to Mark when I was putting my scooter there." Kit and I go upstairs so we can both be near when she discovers the scooter. She messes about as she normally does then says, "Goodnight," and pulls the covers up.

We can hear an 'oh' followed by, "Mum I found my scooter, it's in my bed."

I reply with a serious face, "What do you mean it's in your bed? Someone stole it." I can see in her face she is trying to gage whether we are playing a joke or not.

She says, "No, it's in my bed."

I jump up dramatically saying, "Someone has put your scooter back in your bed? I need to phone the police." Her face immediately turns to panic and then I say, "Joking. We put it there. The scooter didn't even leave the house today. It wasn't at the bike rack, nobody stole it." She half-laughs and then runs into Kit's arms who is sitting on the bed. She's a mixture of relief, embarrassment and disbelief.

I then say to her, "Your face was a picture." And then she laughs and then buries her face into Kit.

Our girl might be the most forgetful unorganised girl ever but she can always, always take a joke and she was able to see the funny side of us putting the scooter in her bed to find.

She says , "Mum do you know that I actually thought someone stole it and then brought it back and put it in my bed."

And I say , "Yeah, I know. I could actually see the panic come over your face as you were trying to piece it all together." I then do an impression of her face and we all laugh. Thankfully she has a sense of humour, otherwise dealing with her unorganised forgetful ways would be much less tolerable.

Chapter 57

Your Wants Come Second

I take the kids to the Scotland rugby game on Saturday at Murrayfield. I'm supposed to get there early to meet some rugby friends at the fan zone before the game and hoping to meet up again after the game. I realise very quickly the day is not going to go as planned. I need to drive because Annie has a cold and isn't feeling great so I can't drag her around using public transport. Traffic is horrendous and we get to the game with ten minutes before kick-off. I miss the meet up in the fan zone. I say to myself, *It's okay, I can meet them afterwards.* Annie's favourite part of the rugby game is eating her sweeties she brought from her Halloween bucket. Once the sweets are finished the boredom sets in pretty quickly. I spend the second half of the game trying to entertain her and watch the game at the same time. After the game, I head to the fan zone to see the rugby gang. It's so busy and Annie is so tiny, it's hard work trapsing through the crowds. On my way to the fan zone, I bump into three of the rugby girls who are current players in the womens team. I stop and have a chat. They ask me how my ribs are and I tell them they are pretty much healed. My first game back playing rugby eight weeks ago and I broke my ribs so haven't been back training since.

They say, "Will you be coming along to watch the game tomorrow?" I instantly feel guilty.

I say, "I can't, the kids have a birthday party and Kit is away in America for work so I need to be on driving duties."

It's funny, I feel like I'm giving a really lame excuse. I realise my vision of going back to rugby and it being like it used to be it far from my reality now. By the time I make my way to the fan zone the kids are well and truly bored and wanting to get home. I spend all of five minutes saying a quick hello before then heading back home with the kids. I think back to how days like these used to look. I just had to organise myself, spend the whole day socialising before the game, during the game and then heading to the pub with no restrictions of when I needed to head home, only thinking about myself. I trained Tuesday night, Thursday night and spent the whole day Sunday on game day, getting there early, staying late, going out on Sunday night. Since I've went back to playing, I've only managed one game before I broke my ribs but it's just such a big commitment and time to take away from things that are already planned with the kids and their social activities. Now the norm is to be second. It's funny how naïve I was, thinking how easy it would be to include that as part of my life the way it once was. Maybe I need to commit to something for myself that is less time-consuming, I know it's important to have something for myself.

Chapter 58

The Constant Nonsense Chatter

Oh my goodness I've just exploded! I have just had enough. My mum is over staying for the week to help as Kit is away working abroad for the week. Trying to get two minutes to have time just to chat to my mum without the kids interrupting with absolute nonsense chatter is impossible. I am absolutely exasperated. It is just constant. Neither of them stops for air. And the constant competition and having to be the best is just so draining. I have literally reached boiling point tonight.

"Riiiighhhhttttt. *Enough!* I can't hear myself think!" I shout. They both look with shocked expressions. "You are going on and on and not even saying anything. I start a conversation with Nana and you both start talking over us. I speak to one of you and other one then speaks louder to drown out the conversation. I'm exhausted by it." Annie goes to interrupt and I quickly shout, "I'm not finished."

She looks up. "Oh."

I continue, looking at Rosie, "Just because I would be talking to Annie does not then mean that I all of a sudden don't love you or you are not as important as her or she is better than you, that's not how life works." I can feel myself going into preaching mode but it's too late, I can't stop myself I keep going, knowing they probably won't be taking a word in but for my own sanity I need to vent. "This is not fun for me, the constant interrupting and nonsense chatter has to stop and talking over each other has to stop. I like to have some quiet moments, little silences are okay, it's normal. When you are not constantly chatting nonsense you are both great company, you are so lovely to be around." I look at Rosie, "You have a great sense of humour and really know how to take a joke. You are also super smart and know so much about interesting things so you could easily talk about those things." I then look at Annie, "And you are really funny and so good at making people laugh."

As I'm talking she then starts saying, "Watch this Mum." And started pulling this wee face where she looks up to the right and raises her eyebrows.

I raise my hands to my head "Annie, I need you to listen just now, not be funny." But she continues with the face and it becomes so apparent to me how little impact my rant is having. I give up. My head is in my hands.

"Right, as of tomorrow, you are both getting new reward charts."

Before I can even finish and say what the reward charts are for they are both cheering, "Yeeaahhh, stickers." I can't say having the rant made me feel better or indeed changed anything but hopefully the reward sticker charts will have some impact. I sat down that night and got the

reward chart pack that I have left in the cupboard from the last time we used the reward charts. The new chart included:
1. I will not interrupt when people are speaking.
2. I will not speak over my sister.
3. I will listen when other people are talking.
4. I will use my quiet voice.
5. I will sit still and use my cutlery at the dinner table (Annie).
6. I will be more aware of constant nonsense chatter and have more quiet time (Rosie).
7. When an adult asks me to do something I will do it without talking back.

The excitement over the rewards charts is unreal as I show them at breakfast table the following morning.

"You get a star for each thing on your chart every day. You only get two reminders. At the end when you get all your stars you then get to choose a big sticker."

"Wow," Annie says. "Look at all the stickers…"

Rosie then spoke right over Annie and Annie says without hesistation, "Rosie I was speaking; you aren't allowed to speak over me."

I say , "That's right, Annie. That's your first reminder Rosie. If you then do it a second time you don't earn your star."

"Okay Mum, we are doing this," replies Rosie. The next few days they try really hard. The dinner table atmosphere is like night and day. Because Rosie isn't just talking constantly it means Annie then isn't trying to compete to talk so there are lovely, normal, peaceful breaks of silence and I am able to chat to my mum and actually hear her reply without the kids talking over us. It is the most relaxed time I have had at dinner in such a long time. Long way it last.

Chapter 59

Parents' Night—What a Difference a Year Makes

"Rosie is just a delight," Mrs Jamieson starts off. I instantly warm to her. She's around my age and speaks with a warm tone. "She is so enthusiastic about everything she does in school and always puts in 100% in her learning tasks…" Mrs Jamieson is only supposed to be on the phone for a ten-minute consultation but she speaks to me for fifty-five minutes. She is so positive and solution focused about Rosie, nothing seems to be a hassle for her. I know Rosie must be intense to have in the class, the same way she's intense to have around the house, but Mrs Jamieson doesn't seem phased by her. She goes on to tell me that she has started a friendship club that she runs in her classroom every Monday. She sits and eats her lunch at her desk and she sets up different boardgames that the kids can play together. Some of the games belong to her when she was a child that she got from her parents' attic. She didn't say it but I did wonder if Rosie was the reason she set the club up. Rosie has continued to struggle with her peer relationships, there's definite improvements but it is still really hard for her. Mrs Jamieson goes on to say, "Rosie has been playing draughts with another girl at the friendship club. Rosie has lost every game and she has taken it so well, saying good game and voicing how amazing the other player is."

I reply , "Oh my God, this makes me so happy. Rosie would not have been able to cope with losing a game when she was in P4. She would have gone off crying at the first loss. We have been working so hard on this with her at home."

Mrs Jamieson replies , "Wow, I would never have known that; you have worked wonders with her then." It is nice to get the acknowledgement from Mrs Jamieson. I go on to tell her that Rosie was due to get her letterbox contact from her birth mum in the next few weeks just in case she becomes unsettled and she will understand why. She went on to tell me that she used to work with birth parents who were writing letters to their kids who had been adopted. I didn't even know there was such a thing. It made me think of Michelle. I really hope she has someone to support her. I finish the phone call and I head downstairs. Rosie is waiting patiently for her update. I start off by telling her how proud I am of all the good work and effort she puts in at school. She's very pleased with herself. I go on to talk about the difference in how she copes when losing a game.

She says , "I shake her hand and say good game Mum."

I say "I know, Mrs Jamieson told me." It's unbelievable to think of the progress she's made in a year.

I say , "So there's always little things to work on. Mrs Jamieson wants you to work on the way you speak to your classmates. Sometimes the things you say can be really hurtful, and not because you mean it but because you aren't aware of how your words can make people feel upset or sad." I gave her the examples that Mrs Jamieson gave me and tried to explain how it makes others feel upset. She seemed to listen and get it. "And the last thing you need to work on is the need to finish first and then shout out to tell the whole class you are finished first. It's really great that you are so smart and work so hard and finish quickly but you need to be aware of what that means for everyone else around you. There are some kids that never finish first because they struggle and every time you do that it pushes you further away from the rest of your class. You have told me how badly you want to make friends with your classmates. Why don't you, instead of announcing to the whole class you are finished and them thinking you are a smart Alec, why not finish quietly and maybe chat quietly to someone at your table or even quietly see if someone needs help?."

"Okay Mum, I will try that." This conversation is so tough. I never want to dent her confidence or enthusiasm for work but I also get why her peers are so rejecting of her at times. I was one of the kids that never finished first in class and I'm certain if Rosie had been in my class and did that after every learning exercise, I would be rolling my eyes and subconsciously making the decision that me and her wouldn't be friends in the playground as her need to tell everyone she's the best wouldn't make me feel good. Comparing P4's parents' consultation is like night and day. Looking back to the issues she was facing compared to how she's managing now is pretty incredible.

Chapter 60

Letterbox Contact #2

As soon as November hits there's an underlying anxiety for all of us. We are all wondering when the letter will arrive, all praying a letter will arrive. It's mid-November and Rosie comes to my bedroom door before school this morning, "Mum when will my letter arrive from my mum?" I look up and I can see that she has a nervous look on her face, whether it's purely because of the anxiety of the letter or if it was anxiety provoking plucking up the courage to ask me, I don't know.

I say, "We don't get an exact date, we are only told November but I will email social work today and see if they know, okay?"

"Okay Mum," she replies and she bounces back downstairs. I have this constant underlying fear that one day a letter might not come. Please, please, please don't let it be this day.

I email the girls' old social worker to see if she knows any info about the letterbox contact that is due. She replies to my email within the hour. *Hi Nell, I've contacted the letterbox contact department. Michelle has sent a card. It should be with you within the next day or so.* Phew, I feel a sense of relief. I often wonder how she's getting on with their sibling. He will be over a year now. I hope she's doing well. Sure enough, the letter arrives the next day. Addressed to Mr and Mrs —classic social work getting the smallest of things wrong. It is a Christmas card that has a family with a dog on the front that writes , *Happy Christmas to all of you.* I open the card and read it and have a wee cry. Right at the start of this journey if someone had told me I would cry when the letter from birth mum would arrive I would have thought they were way off the mark. I had never anticipated to be so affected by the loss they all felt. Christmas can be such a hard time of year for some people, I can only imagine how she must feel on Christmas Day. It's always so bittersweet. What is a real highlight for us, is another loss for Michelle.

Rosie comes in from school and we give her the letter. She says straight away, "Aww that's us on the front, even Angus."

I can see an instant relief in her. It's like a weight has been lifted because if Michelle has written to her then to her she feels good knowing Michelle has been thinking about her and is also alive and safe.

She says , "Why are there no photos of my brother this time?."

I say , "Oh I don't know; you might get some in the next letter." I can see the little clogs of her brain working. She is probably wondering if he is still living with her birth mum or if he has been taken into care. We don't get to know any information like that. The card is signed from Mum and Josh so dare I say it but at least she knew he was alive.

The next few days, Rosie talks more about Michelle. The more Rosie openly talks about her mum the more confused Annie seems to be. The more confused Annie is the more unsettled she becomes. The more unsettled she becomes the more challenging her behaviour is, the ongoing cycle we come up against as adoptive parents. She has started to become more deviant again and say no to *everything* and has been back to getting up during the night, playing around for hours. I watch her confused expression when Rosie talks about her birth mum.

We are at the dinner table and Rosie says, "I lived in a lot of different houses when I was with my mum. Will we move house?"

I go to answer but before I can talk Annie jumps in, "No Rosie we are not moving. I don't want to. We have our house and Mummy Nell and Mummy Kit and school." Her facial expression has a sense of desperation. She looks at me, "Right Mum?."

I reply, "We might move house one day, but you will never have to live with anyone else. We are your family and will always take care of you so you never have to worry about having to ever move in with anyone new ever again. We are your forever family."

She replies, "Yeah so we don't need another mummy."

I say, "Michelle will always be your birth mum and we are your adopted mums. You were born in Michelle's tummy and she wasn't able to take care of you so now you live with us and we will take care of you forever." She seems satisfied with my explanation but of course it's so hard to really know what's going on in her head. The age gap of four and a half years can make these things really quite hard to navigate. Their experiences are so different. Rosie remembers her birth mum, and rightly so should be able to talk openly about her and her life experiences before coming to live with us, eight years is a long time after all. It's trying to navigate Annie through these times so the story can make sense to her without her sitting worrying that she might be going to live with 'another mummy' and be taken away from what she knows. I think it's so important that they both know and understand their life story, the age gap just makes it much more complicated for us. As long as we keep an open dialogue, the older Annie gets the more it will make sense to her.

Chapter 61

Rosie's First Rugby Match

It's seven-forty-five on Sunday morning and I creep downstairs thinking everyone is still in bed. I get the fright of my life when Rosie pops her little head up from the couch, "Hi Mum."

"Oh my God," I say.

"What a fright," she says. "Look at me." And she jumps up with a big smile on her face. She has her full rugby strip on, even her socks are pulled right up.

I say, "Love it, you look great." She follows me round the kitchen every step I take and is chatting constantly. *So much for my quiet, chilled morning,* I think to myself.

"Mum I'm going to run so fast. Mum I'm going to score a try. Mum I'm going to do a big tackle. Mum I'm going to do a cartwheel when we win. Mum, Mum, Mum…."

Kick-off is at ten-thirty a.m. We all get wrapped up and make our way to the game. Rosie is now quieter in the car on the way there. I think her nerves are now setting in, her narrative has now changed from what she was saying this morning. "As long as I have fun, that's what matters," she says.

I reply, "Yeah, no pressure. It's your first game and remember there are a lot of rules, just enjoy it."

She says, "Yeah but I know the rules."

I say, "Rosie there are so many rules to rugby. I still don't understand all of them and I've been playing for years. You are the new person on the team, people won't expect you to know everything."

"Yeah, but I do know a lot."

"Yes, you do know the important rules, but you have a lot to learn." She really struggles to be in a position where she doesn't know best. Both Kit and I are often trying to explain to her that there will be lots of situations in life where she won't be the one who knows best and trying to explain it's okay to ask more questions and say she doesn't know is normal. The struggle is real. We are using the expression, 'no one likes a smart Alec'. She is now copying the expression when she hears her sister saying she knows how to do something that she actually doesn't. It's a work in progress trying to help Rosie to be more self-aware of when she is doing it.

We get to the pitch and her team have gathered and are warming up.

I say, "Put your boots on now and I will keep your bag for you." She starts trying to put her boots on but is seriously struggling. I say, "You need to put your thumb at the back and then push your foot in." She is choosing not to listen and keeps forcing her foot in without using her thumb and the back on the boot is folding and she then isn't able to pull it back up. I repeatedly say, "Rosie, use your thumb." She is getting more and more frustrated and I know the signs are coming, she's about to go into a complete meltdown.

I bend down quickly and I put my thumb into the boot, "Now push." Her foot then goes in with no problem. I then say, "Now just do the same with the other boot."

She screams back, "I can't, it won't work." She's nearly crying, so I quickly decide that this moment in time is not a good time to have a learning moment managing her frustrations. I repeat the same thing with her right boot, and then she's tying her laces and still franticly looking around. She's obviously nervous.

I say, "Just enjoy it, there's no pressure."

She looks up, "Okay Mum." She puts her gum guard in and gives a big smile and she runs over to join her team mates who are playing games for warm-up. Kit, Annie, Angus and I all sit at the stand. It feels exciting.

Kit says, "Do you want a coffee?." The home team have big pots of tea and coffee available but you need money to buy some.

I say, "I didn't bring any money." Rooky mistake for first time supporters. It's freezing too. The game kicks off so we walk down to be closer. She's on the sub bench to begin with but after a few minutes she gets on. Kit and I get so into it.

We are shouting at the sidelines, "Good hands, back yourself, brilliant tackle." Rosie, as expected, is a bit scared when the other team comes running towards her and to be fair to her the other side is all boys who look much bigger than her team. She gradually gets more into it and she makes her first tackle. We cheer like crazy at the sideline, "Yes, brilliant tackle Rosie." She looks over and I give her a big thumbs up. She gives us a thumbs up back. It's great to see her enjoying it.

The final whistle blows and she comes running over. "Well done." And we high five.

She says , "Mum did you see when I tackled that boy and he landed on my leg?"

I say, "Yeah it was a great tackle." She looks really happy with herself. Her smile grows even bigger when she finds out that the players get hot dogs and cupcakes.

At this point Annie then pipes up, "Mum I want to play rugby now."

I say , "Why's that?"

She replies, "Because I want a cupcake."

I reply, "Of course you do," as I smile at her.

Chapter 62

Two Weeks of the Reward Charts

It's been two weeks since we started the reward charts. It's unbelievable how invested they get in gaining stickers. The difference I've noticed in them not interrupting others and listening more is huge. Don't get me wrong, they still need reminders, as all kids do and there have been some nights where they haven't gotten stars for some things but in general it has been so helpful. Just having more quiet time so I can then have more head space and not feel like I'm constantly in sensory overload is bliss.

I say to Rosie, "I look forward to sitting down at the dinner table now because it's so much more pleasant without the constant interrupting and you now sit back and listen to other people chatting. It's so nice."

She smiles and says, "Mum I've been trying really hard with it."

I reply, "I can tell, the difference is amazing." The most notable thing is that because Rosie has stopped with the constant chatter, Annie doesn't try and compete to get her chance to talk. I've noticed she is much more relaxed and happier to sit quietly and contently in her own little world now just eating her food. Whereas before, she would be moving around constantly and trying to speak to be heard and not relaxed at all. Long may the rewards chart make an impact. When I think about the rewards charts it takes me back to my time when I worked in MST. I did a lot of rewards charts with parents for lots of different kids and learned a lot about behaviour management strategies in that job. I honestly don't think I would be doing this well if it hadn't been for the valuable experience of working in MST. It's true that your previous experiences really do make you who you are.

Chapter 63

Play Date

I'm driving home like a mad woman trying to make sure I get to Annie on-time for pick up at two-thirty p.m. I wiz into the driveway, run into the house, grab her scooter, the lead and the dog and scoot on round to the school, just in time for pick up. This is my daily routine from Monday to Thursday. As we are walking home, Annie's classmate is walking behind us with her mum.

Annie turns and shouts, "Emily, hi." And she waves franticly. She then looks at me and says, "I made a new friend today Mum." She scoots ahead chatting with Emily and I hang back and chat with Emily's mum who I know from chatting to whilst doing drop-off and pick up and they live just round the street from us. They are a really lovely family. Emily's brother is eight years old and such a polite little boy. I often have thought about how nice and 'normal' they are as a family. They always look happy and thriving. We get to just outside Emily's house and she shouts to her mum

"Mummy can Annie please come for a play date?"

Annie's face lights up and she looks to me, "Aww can we Mum?" Emily's Mum then says, "You are welcome just now if you are free."

Annie then says, "I have an idea, how about we play with the toys and the mummies sit and drink coffee?."

Emily's mum laughs and replies, "You have the plans sorted."

I say, "I will just nip round to the house to put the dog and the scooter away and come back round." Annie is beside herself.

She screams, "Yeah, play date." It's lovely and relaxed when I go back round. Annie and Emily and upstairs playing and I sit at the lovely big dining table in the kitchen. We spend around an hour. I chatted with Emily's mum and the kids came back and forward for snacks and to check in. Annie is so well behaved. We then get ready to leave so we can be at home in time for Rosie getting back from basketball. Annie says, "Thanks for letting me over to play." And we wave bye and walk back to our own house just around the corner. We walk hand in hand.

I say, "Thank you for being such a good girl at Emily's house."

She replies, "You're welcome."

I say, "Santa will be so happy with you."

She looks up smiling, "Yes 'cause I'm on the nice list." We get home and I start making dinner. Rosie comes home from basketball and she is happy to start doing her homework at the kitchen table. Annie takes it upon herself to get her colouring book and pens and sits at the table too. I think about how different life is, how different I am, how different they are. I used to look at Emily and her family and hope that our little family could be like them one day: a happy, loving, family. This time last year if we had been invited on a spur of the moment play date, I honestly don't think I would have gone because I would have been too nervous about Annie's behaviour and more to the point my ability to manage it but today has made me see just how much we have all grown. We are more like Emily's family than I had realised. Even just being in the kitchen making food and watching them sit doing their tasks quietly chatting. Chatting not for attention but just relaxed chatting and giggling. This is what we have been striving for. We are a 'normal' family.

Chapter 64

I'm the Star that Guides You

It is Annie's nativity at school today.. She is the star. She has been practising for weeks but every time I asked her about it she kept saying, "It's a surprise."

I would hear her in the bath or when playing with her toys and she didn't think anyone was watching or could hear and she would sing some lines of the songs.

I say to her, "Who is playing Mary?"

To which she replies , "Mary is a boy."

I then say , "Is baby Jesus a doll or is someone playing baby Jesus?"

She says , "We don't have a baby Jesus in our show." I am imagining what chaos it must be for the teacher to organise and get twenty-three Primary ones to perform such a show, especially since Annie really doesn't appear to grasp the basic concept of the story and the characters. I couldn't wait to see it in action. Kit and I walk round to get there early so we can get front row. Other parents had the same idea but luckily there are a few seats left on the front row and we get them. The stage is all done up lovely. They have really put in such an effort. The headteacher gives a little welcome introduction. I still don't like her very much for the way she spoke to Rosie that day. All the children then start walking in and go up on stage. The costumes are just brilliant. Annie is last in the line and she has the cutest star outfit on.

She spots us in the audience and shouts, "Mummy Kit, Mummy Nell," with a big smile on her face as she is waving franticly.

I am welling up already and it hasn't even started yet. Then the first song is played and she proudly beams out all the words. She's watching us the whole time. Then it's her turn to do her part.

She walks right to the front of the stage and says, "I'm the big star that will guide you all to the baby Jesus." Then they sing a song about following the star and she runs around the stage pretending to guide everyone. She is in her element. When the audience all applaud at the end she is delighted. I give her a thumbs up and she does it back. I'm so proud of her.

That night I'm sitting at the dinner table with Rosie and Annie and I say to Rosie, "Do you want to see the videos I took of Annie's nativity?"

Rosie says straight away, "No I don't want to see her videos." Rosie then tries to talk continuously moving on to something unrelated to Annie's nativity about her brownies Christmas party. I ignore her reaction at that point and continue talking to Annie about her nativity and Annie enjoys watching the videos I took of her.

Rosie then says, "You can't even sing."

I say, "That's enough. There is no need for cruel words."

"It's true," she replies. I then feel the rage rise inside me.

I say, "The only truth here is that you are saying all of these cruel things because you are jealous." She gives me a look and remains silent.

She walks away from the dinner table and Annie looks up to me and asks, "Was I not good in my show Mum?"

I say, "You were a shining star darling. You were amazing. Sometimes people say things just to be mean when they are feeling jealous."

She replies, "Aww that sister." I laugh.

She says that because she often hears me say, 'Aww that girl', when Rosie hasn't done something properly. Rosie goes off to brownies and doesn't say anything else about it.

That night when she gets home and Annie is sound asleep, I say to her "I know it was rubbish for you that you didn't get to do the nativity when you were in primary one and you feel sad about it because it's an experience you missed out on but that is not Annie's fault."

She butts in, "I know it's not her fault."

I continue, "Do you remember when it was your dance show and Annie was shouting and cheering in the audience and shouting, 'that's my sister' and how happy it made you feel?"

She replies, "Yes."

I say, "Do you want to be a person that people look forward to sharing their successes with because you cheer them on and are happy for them or do you want to be the person that people avoid sharing good news with because you will put a negative spin on it and not make them feel good?"

She replies, "I want people to tell me good things."

I say, "Then you need to work on hiding your jealously and showing an interest in others."

I continue, "I actually think once you practice being happy for Annie in different situations you will enjoy being a big sister that supports her sister and you will love it if you are someone she looks for straight away to share her successes."

She says, "Okay Mum I will try."

I know it's going to be easier said than done for her. There is definitely the normal sibling rivalry between the two of them but then there's the added complexity of Rosie's first few years of missing certain milestones added on. It's the next morning, we are walking round to school and we meet Emily from Annie's class and her mum and brother on the way round.

Emily's mum says, "How was the nativity? I am going this morning."

Rosie quickly answers, "It was amazing. Annie and Emily were really good."

Emily's mum says, "Oh amazing. I can't wait to see it." Rosie looks over and I give her a wink and she smiles back.

Chapter 65

Someday is Here

It's -6 outside. The coldest winter we have had in a long time. Kit is away with work so I have to take the girls with me to walk Angus. We get all wrapped up in our jackets and hats and scarfs and I give Annie the head torch and tell her she can lead us through the field tonight. She's excited to be the walk leader. Our house is right beside the field which is super handy so I don't even have to put Angus on the lead. We are literally in the field for five minutes and Annie face plants on the icy path and is crying saying, "I'm just so cold." I abandon the walk sooner than expected. Annie is right, it is just too cold to be out here. We all run back and get into our pjs to get warm and cosy.

I'm sitting on the couch with Rosie on one side of me cuddling in and Annie and Angus on the other all sharing the same cosy blanket. *Christmas Chronicles 2* is on the TV and they are sitting watching intently. They both have their Christmas pjs on and I have my Christmas onesie on. The Christmas tree lights are sparkling in the corner of my eye and I can see the ice glistening on the grass from the bifold doors. I have this overwhelming feeling of happiness. When I think back to what the girls were both like when they first came to live with us, it's like night and day. They weren't able to sit down and watch a movie for five minutes never mind sit still and cuddled up for a full movie. There was no way poor Angus would go near Annie because he was so frightened she would hurt him. He's now sprawled right over her knees and his little eyes are just looking at me. If he could talk, I'm sure he would be telling me how comfortable and cosy he was cuddling up with the pack. I sit there thinking about the difference. I can't believe the change when I look back and reflect over the last eighteen months and think about everything we have been through. We have all changed, grown and adapted so much in that short time. We have all had to learn about each other, grow to love each other, deal with the loss of our old lives and find ways to laugh even when it's been really tough. Don't get me wrong, I know there are still tough days to come but they are fewer and less intense than before. I'm content in my reflective thoughts and then Annie pulls me right back to the present moment by saying out of the blue, "Mum I just farted and it smells."

We start waving the blanket and Rosie is shouting, "Yuck that's disgusting." And Angus is grunting because he has been disturbed and isn't happy with the pack.

I am laughing whilst saying, "How can such a bad smell come out such a tiny body?" Annie is doubled over giggling now. This was a moment of realisation. This is the someday I have been waiting for. The day where we feel like an ordinary family. I never imagined this moment would come by sitting in my onesie and Annie doing a smelly fart would have sealed the deal, but life has a funny way of playing out sometimes. Wait until I tell Kit this one, she is going to think I've gone crazy.

THE END